JOYS FROM HOME

by

PEGGY SIMPSON

A book of joyous and serious thoughts for you to pick up and read anytime. . . .

with a plus

A recipe for something good to enjoy along the way.

Food for thought;
A thought for food

QUALITY PUBLICATIONS
P.O. BOX 1060
ABILENE, TEXAS 79604
(915) 677-6262

ISBN: 0-89137-441-8

DEDICATION

to: John
My love and my encourager

ACKNOWLEDGMENTS

My thanks to several friends who read and helped with my manuscript and encouraged me to keep on keeping on: Patty L. Dugger, Barbara Ellis, Beverly Gardner and Mary Helen Lowry.

This book includes several quotes who are unknown to me; therefore, I did not know to whom credit should be given. My thanks to you and your most appropriate statements.

My greatest appreciation goes to my husband, John, whose help and encouragement (and sometimes, criticism) pushed me to the finish line. He always proofed my writing and checked my spelling but mostly he looked for misplaced apostrophes. His tongue in cheek philosophy concerning problems in the world and the written word is: "The main problem in our world today is the fact that there are armies of illiterate people running loose with paper and pencil in hand, armed with apostrophes. They are aimed like the javelin and thrown any and everywhere there is a word ending in 's'."

If you should, by some slip of a pen point, find a misplaced apostrophe somewhere in this book, please know that it found its way in after John's proofing.

Peggy Simpson

All scripture references are from the New International Bible.
Typists: Janet Montgomery and Suzy Mussard.

INTRODUCTION

Not long after *Hospitality - In the Spirit of Love* was written I had an idea for another book. This is it!

I wish to call it *Joys From Home*. It is a collection of true, human interest stories with morals. Also, very good recipes are included. It is a book that the whole family can enjoy, especially women. There are serious pieces as well as fun stories. In many of them, I take a look at myself and see . . . what I see will make other women feel good about themselves. I hope the Joys from My Home will become your joys also.

Peggy Simpson

TABLE OF CONTENTS

Recipe Index Page Number

FIRST IMPRESSIONS

Matthew 5:16 "Let your light so shine before men, that they may see your good works, and glorify your Father which is in heaven."

Opportunities to make new friends are exciting for me. Such an opportunity comes with the writing of this book. As you read and get to know me through these pages, I'll be keeping my fingers crossed in the hope that we become fast and true friends.

Speaking of making new friends, we were privileged to make a trip to the World's Fair while it was in Tennessee. We loved it! On our last day there, we enjoyed a late lunch at the International Buffet on the third floor of the Candy Factory. The place was lovely with large, round dining tables with linen tablecloths and napkins, each table seating six or eight people. We were the first to be seated at ours, and just as we were about to begin eating, a couple, middle-aged woman and younger man, were placed with us.

In the few seconds it took to pick out seeds and eat a bite of watermelon, I managed a quick layman's analysis of the two strangers.

My first thought was, "What have we here? An older woman and younger man — a provoking thought, to say the least! I've read about situations like this!"

The woman had a bit of scowl on her face and the man didn't look any too friendly either. They had probably had a tiff, I thought. I wondered whether they would even speak to me if I made the first effort. Well, I'd never know if I didn't try.

"Hello," I said, "Where are you from?" (This is always a terrific way to get a conversation going.)

The young man replied, "Spokane, Washington," in none too friendly a manner. This was our opening; so I asked the obvious, "How do you like the Fair?"

He answered, hardly looking up, "After Seattle and New York, I can't say much for it."

"We think it's great! . . . and exciting, and feel so proud to have it in the South and near enough that we could drive up. Didn't you like the United States Pavilion and that marvelous film and the musical 'Sing Tennessee'?"

The woman spoke for the first time and said, "We haven't seen that yet. We only arrived yesterday and haven't really had time to see very much."

I brightened at the bit of conversation from her and pushed my luck a little further with, "You're a long way from home. Did you come just for the Fair?"

I suppose she could sense that I was not the enemy because her features softened and she began to talk.

In only a few minutes, while we ate our lunch, she told us that they were mother and son. She and her husband had planned this trip several months ago for their son's graduation from Engineering School at the University of Washington. A month and a half ago, her husband was stricken with a form of cancer that took his life in only two weeks. He had been buried two and a half weeks before. The other children insisted that she and this boy take the trip as planned. They were touring the United States by commercial airlines and had already been to Florida and New York. After about four days in the Knoxville area, they were headed for New Orleans. It was with much difficulty that she was able to travel at all, much less enjoy the scenery.

We talked for as long as we had time. Since my husband and I had to join our tour group and leave for home, we said goodbye to our "Fair" friends and wished them well with God's blessings.

My thoughts since that encounter have been: "Peggy, from now on, please try not to draw unfavorable conclusions about people with your first impressions. Try to get to know them first; then, think what you will."

So it is with me . . . and you.

DESSERT SURPRISE

Wash and hull a pint of fresh strawberries. Split or cut up. Mix with 1½ c. miniature marshmallows. Let set overnight. Before serving, mix with small carton of whipped topping (8 oz.).

Serve this over slice of pound cake, angel food cake or plain layer cake. Very good and quick to prepare.

FAITH

Galatians 5:22,23 "But the fruit of the Spirit is love, joy, peace, patience, kindness, goodness, faithfulness, gentleness and self-control. Against such things there is no law."
Luke 17:6 "He replied, 'if you have faith as small as a mustard seed, you can say to this mulberry tree, be uprooted and planted in the sea,' and it will obey you."

Faith is a virtue that all children possess. It can be easily destroyed, during the growing up years, if we are not ever so careful. The youth of today blame their lack of faith on their parents. They say we have double standards. I am sure this situation is true many, many times. I do not like double standards any more than the most rebellious young man or woman does. Watching while others say "do this and do that" while they, themselves, do just the opposite . . . can trigger off a hatred button in a person and cause him to dump every virtue he ever possessed and start him miserably downhill, hating everything in the path. We do not impress or influence anyone with a lack of faith or with hatred. It shortens our life span and loses us our place in heaven.

Children imitate as they grow. They learn how to deceive and hate from their parents and others with whom they are in close contact. Hate and deception have to be taught as do love and trusting.

Careless words and devilish deeds sown before a child take root and grow. Not of themselves but with our help. If we set bad examples, the first thing we know, we have a rebellious young man or woman on our hands, screaming back into our ears. We have reaped our harvest. Sixteen or seventeen years of cultivating a tender mind reaps us either wheat or tares.

We can learn so much from children. They have perfect faith and complete confidence in those they love. Their trust and faith is natural and has such appealing simplicity. It is our influence and ugliness that mars a child's trustworthiness.

We can learn from children. While we are supplied daily lessons in love, trust, patience, and faith from children, let us strive to make ourselves worthy of their trust.

The goal of any criticism we make of our children is to leave them with the feeling they have been helped and that we have faith in that goodness.

POTATO-CHEESE CHOWDER

3 T. melted margarine
3 medium potatoes, peeled and cubed
1 medium onion, diced
1/4 t. salt
paprika
3 c. milk, scalded
1 8 oz. pkg. American cheese slices, diced
Assorted crackers (optional)

In 3 qt. saucepan, melt butter; add potatoes, onion, salt, and 1/2 t. paprika; cook until vegetables are lightly browned and tender (about 30-45 minutes on medium or low heat), stirring frequently. Add milk and cheese; cook, stirring constantly until mixture is hot and cheese is melted and smooth. To serve, spoon chowder into four soup bowls; sprinkle with paprika. Serve with crackers if you like. Delicious!!!

MOTIVATION

Psalm 62:11,12 "One thing God has spoken, two things have I heard: That you, O God, are strong, and that you, O Lord, are loving. Surely you will reward each person according to what he has done."

Once, after completing six weeks of class work where the student was kept busy writing, talking, and showing ways of accomplishing the goal which was mentioned at the beginning of the study, it dawned on me that I work on command. In other words, it does not take much to motivate me. There we were, working our heads off, actually creating the instructor's work for him. At the end of six weeks, we were awarded a large button which read, "I FEEL TERRIFIC!" But actually, I didn't feel terrific at all. I felt drained and weak and done-in. I even felt as if maybe I had paid out a great deal of money for nothing. In fact, I felt much like someone I heard of the other day who had gone through the agony of losing his teeth and getting used to dentures, only to gargle, rinse, and flush one time too many. He lost his new expensive teeth down the toilet.

While thinking how little it sometimes takes to motivate one person to do his or her work, fifty "I FEEL TERRIFIC!" buttons would not do the same for someone else.

Corporations and industry probably spend more on ways to motivate their workers than they pay out in salaries. And to this day motivation is a mystery. Few of us concentrate fully on our jobs. We devote only a small fraction of our attention to what we are doing and to getting the job done. Occasionally though, someone finds himself motivated to focus and think totally on a project, with the result being a feeling of knowing the job has been done well, and that the finished product has gone far beyond the routine performance. Often, motivation with some person involves no more than a check at the end of the day or week or month or a pat on the back, or maybe just a word of encouragement. It would be great if we could ever find out what we could do to cause someone elso to want to do his or her best, that is, how to connect work and motives so that the task itself becomes exciting.

A few months ago, I was in the check-out line at the grocery. To help pass the time, I began to notice what other people had in their carts. I was amazed as I recognized the couple in the line next to me and observed the large number of TV dinners they were planning to eat. It was, for the most part, the kind containing a patty of meat that reminds me of the canine special burger, a teaspoonful of dehydrated potatoes, and the nickel-sized green peas.

I started counting the number of dinners in their basket. Just as I got to twenty-nine, the couple noticed me. I spoke to them and tried to take on a look of "that you should prefer grainsburgers twice a day for weeks is absolutely normal" but said, "was there a special buy on TV dinners?"

They looked at me for a few seconds. Then with the force of a small tornado, the wife jabbed her husband in the ribs with her elbow. and he quickly said, with a pained smile, "There was no special sale today, we just love TV dinners!"

Motivation, sometimes, is like a jab in the ribs. Sometimes it is a case of survival, as in the case of the frog who found himself caught in a very deep rut on a country road. Though his friends tried with all their might to help him get out, their efforts were to no avail. At last they left him in the deepest despair.

The very next day one of these friends was hopping along that country road, and whom did he meet but the very same frog who the day before had been hopelessly stuck in the rut of the road.

"Well, I'll be a tree toad," said the friendly frog; "I thought you were stuck in that rut for good and couldn't get out."

"That's right, I couldn't," the first frog said, "but a truck came along . . . and I had to!!!"

It is exciting to ponder over just what would happen if all of us, even for one day, used the total power of all our resources, which we usually use just when we think we have to.

MY FAVORITE BROCCOLI CASSEROLE

2-10 oz. pkgs. frozen broccoli
1 can mushroom soup
1 c. shredded cheddar cheese
1 onion, minced
2 eggs, beaten
1 c. mayonnaise
1 T. savory

Cook broccoli, drain and cool. Mix all other ingredients. Add broccoli. Pour into greased oblong casserole baking dish. Top with bread crumbs. Bake 350 degrees for 45 minutes.

PEACH DELIGHT

Crust:
1 c. flour
1 stick butter or margarine
1 c. chopped nuts

Mix and press into 13" x 9" Pyrex dish. Bake 350 degrees for 20-25 minutes. Cool completely.

Filling:
8 oz. cream cheese
½ c. sugar
1 small box vanilla instant pudding
1 tall can evaporated milk
8 oz. whipped topping

Mix first four ingredients well. Fold in whipped topping. Spread on cooled crust.

Topping: Cover top of filling with can of Peach Pie Filling.

GERMAN POTATO SALAD

Served with bratwurst

Dressing:
2 T. vinegar
½ t. dry mustard
¼ t. celery seed
1/8 t. pepper
1 egg beaten
2 T. sugar

Salad:
4 slices bacon
1½ c. water
½ c. milk
6 bratwurst
¼ c. sliced green onions
1 t. instant beef bullion or 1 cube
1½ c. instant potato flakes

In small saucepan, combine all dressing ingredients — cook over medium heat stirring constantly, until thickened. Set aside.

In large skillet, fry bacon until crisp — remove bacon from pan; crumble and set aside. Add onions to bacon drippings and cook until tender. Stir in water and beef bullion; bring to rolling boil — remove from heat. Add milk and potato flakes, stirring until combined. Add bacon and dressing; stir until well mixed — keep hot.

Grill or steam bratwurst until thoroughly cooked. Split each bratwurst lengthwise not cutting through completely. Spread open. Top each with about ½ c. hot potato salad. Serve immediately. One of our favorites.

Tip for Cole Slaw

Make your favorite slaw. If you don't already, add a slice or shredded peeled turnip or raw chopped cauliflower — when ready to serve, heat 1/2 c. coarsely chopped peanuts in 1 T. butter in small skillet or microwave. Add to slaw. Toss. Adds a delightful flavor.

ANGER

1 Timothy 2:8 "I will therefore that men pray everywhere, lifting up holy hands, without wrath and doubting."

We are told from God's word that Christians are to be Christlike, loving and gentle. We can be firm with our persuasion and yet be loving and gentle. We cannot read of a single instance where, when Christ was teaching the great truths, He was angry at the person to whom He was speaking. We cannot imagine the people whom Christ or the Apostles were persuading to become Christians becoming such if they were taught in screams and anger. We are taught to be humble when we try to teach others.

One Lord's Day, a few years ago, we were visiting a congregation and were seated next to a young mother and her son. During the worship service, while the sermon was being delivered, the minister, while making his views and opinion on the subject known, was banging his fist and talking in harsh, loud tones. The little boy who was sitting on my right, and who had been sitting very attentively, suddenly looked at his mother and whispered aloud, "Mama, why is he so mad?"

In all truthfulness, I must confess, I did not hear too much of the remainder of the sermon. I sat there and let my mind wander through the many sermons and parables that Christ taught while here on earth, trying to think if He ever got angry at the people gathered to hear Him.

We cannot drive people to the truth, only animals can be driven. People have to be taught and led. "He shall feed his flock like a shepherd: he shall gather the lambs with his arm, and carry them in his bosom, and shall gently lead those that are with young." This is a perfect picture of patience and tenderness, certainly not anger.

COOK'S NOTE

A small piece of sponge saturated with milk or egg white makes a handy pastry brush for glazing breads and pastries. The sponge spreads the glaze easily and smoothly without tearing the surface.

CORNBREAD SALAD

1 med. skillet cooked, crusty cornbread, crumbled
2 small onions, sliced
$1/2$ lb. bacon, crisp and crumbled
3 tomatoes, chopped
1 med. bell pepper, chopped
$1/2$ c. sweet pickle relish

Layer in salad bowl beginning with cornbread. After all layers are completed, top with the following dressing.

Dressing: $1\,1/2$ c. mayonnaise
$1/2$ c. sweet pickle relish
2 T. sugar

Mix and drizzle over salad. Cover with plastic wrap and refrigerate for 2 hours or more. Serves 6.

WHEN THE LAST ONE LEAVES HOME

Psalm 113:9 "He settles the barren woman in her home as a happy mother of children."

My husband and I thought we had been through one of the longest days of our lives the day our oldest son left home, moving to another town to take a job and "be on his own". He had stayed at home longer than most boys stay, and we thought the length of time was good, feeling as we do about strengthening family life and believing that most children, especially boys, are not mature at seventeen when they graduate from high school. I suppose, however, when ever a child waves goodbye and says, "So long", to the life he's known since making his debut into this world, we still feel very emotional. Dad has to shake son's hand and say, "Good luck, we love you", and "Let us hear from you," while mom has to hug and hug and kiss with a peck on the cheek, accomplishing the hardest part of all, getting out the proverbial scissors and cutting the apron strings as the son drives slowly away, smiling bravely and waving courageously. This experience occurs when the first one leaves.

This "letting go" is hard. The mind tells you this is the way life should be and you would not want it any other way, while the heart is hurting and the tears just will not stop. Regardless of the pain, we realize, of course that a child is not truly educated until he learns independence.

Then comes the time when the youngest is ready to "try his wings." He has always been more homeloving, never liking to be somewhere else more than at home. He likes to cook, therefore has stayed in the kitchen and near where I am. In addition he has always been a very good, gentle boy, honoring his father and mother in every way. The times he has been disobedient and rebellious have been few, since he is generally enthusiastic about everything good.

At this moment a story comes to mind that has nothing to do with my subject, but I think I'll tell it anyway. I thought of it when writing about our son's enthusiasm.

Once, during a Bible lesson at school, when he was in the 6th grade, the scripture was read where Abraham "knew" his wife and Isaac was born. Someone in the class wanted to know why the term "knew" was always used right before a child was born. The teacher explained this mystery to the class and maybe this was the beginning of sex education in school. That afternoon, as our "knowledgeable" 6th grader bounded off the school bus, just a glance would indicate that he was excited.

"Mama, I'll bet you that today I learned something from the Bible, that you don't know."

I was quick to tell him that was certainly possible and most likely. "What did you learn?", I asked.

He then exclaimed, "I'll bet you don't know what the Bible means when it says someone 'knew' his wife."

I confessed that I did know what that meant. Clearly to our son's disappointment, he said, "Whew, man, am I glad I don't have to explain that to you!"

This son of ours grew to be six and one half feet tall and two hundred and twenty-six pounds of joy to have around. His laughter has always been infectious. When Charles laughs, he has such a happy laughter, everybody around laughs.

Being a home-loving boy, he chose to go to the local university for his first two years, reasoning that no matter which field he chose to enter he could get what he needed his first two years at home. In order to get the subjects needed in his chosen field he realized that he would have to transfer to another school later on.

The week before leaving, we began to have to pack and make lists and wash and iron and mend and make ready. He was to begin classes on the 30th of December. The week flew by. We were so aware of the void that was sure to come. We all seemed to be overly kind to one another (much more than normal) and overly considerate. Often I heard: "Mom, if you will make a grocery list, I'll be happy to get groceries for you." And, "Mom, I'll be in town today, anything you need?"

On Friday evening, our older son came home so that he could help Chuck move on Saturday morning. Then, after a big breakfast when nobody was particularly hungry, Chuck left.

To fill the emptiness left in my heart the rest of the day, I was ever so grateful for the dirty dishes. Washing dishes by hand is a blessing if a person has things on his or her heart and mind. It is the best place in the world to think and recall fond memories and pray.

Cutting the apron strings hurts ever so much more than cutting the umbilical cord at birth. We give birth, rejoice at having sons, go through years of raising them, teaching them, loving them and disciplining them, hoping and praying that we are doing a fair job so that when the time comes, they will be able to walk into the world . . . able to live in the world but hopefully not allow the world to live in them. We know fully the time will come when we will be able to let go, smiling bravely and wishing them well.

This cutting loose our son was accomplished, and we somehow made it through the longest day in our lives . . . up to that point, at any rate.

There were adjustments to make! Listening for the door to open . . . hearing, "Mom, I'm home, what's for dinner?" Or, simply, "Mom, I'm home." We began to realize that if the necessary adjustments are made, it will be at least two months before we hear any of these familiar sounds. We can go ahead and eat as early as we please, for there is no one for whom to wait dinner. We can go through the house as many times as we please, looking for dirty clothes and the "other sock" to go with the one in the wash . . . there won't be any.

We can go into the bathroom as many times as we please, looking for towels left on the floor. The towel will be hanging where we left it earlier. We can plan on watching all our favorite shows on TV; there won't be any coins tossed to see if it's M.A.S.H. reruns or the Evening News. We can watch whatever we wish . . . and suddenly discover that M.A.S.H. was what we preferred all the time because we could catch the News at a later time.

Special Wishes to Both Our Sons

May you behave and conduct your lives in such a way that your good name will always be admired and cherished. You may lose the ring we bought for your graduation; it can be replaced. Your name, however, can never be replaced. It was clean and bright the day we gave it to you and worthy for you to wear. When your dad got it from his father, there was no dishonor connected with it. We pray you will guard it wisely. Never let shame or black marks discolor it. You will be glad you kept it clean when the time comes to give it to your sons or daughters. We love you so very much.

OUR TASKS

"Your task is to build a better world," God said. I answered, "How? This world is such a large, vast place . . . so complicated now. And I so small and useless am, there's nothing I can do."

But God in all His wisdom said, "JUST BUILD A BETTER YOU."
Author Unknown

SIMPSON'S BANANAS FOSTER

1 pint vanilla ice cream
1/3 c. packed dark brown sugar
3 T. butter or margarine
1/4 c. golden raisins
2 medium bananas, sliced
1/3 c. pecans, chopped

Remove ice cream from freezer; let stand at room temperature to soften slightly, about 10 minutes. Meanwhile, in 10 inch skillet over low heat, heat brown sugar and butter until mixture is melted, stirring frequently. Add raisins and bananas; cook 5 minutes or until fruit is heated through and through, gently turning fruit.

Spoon ice cream into four dessert dishes; top with banana mixture. Sprinkle with chopped pecans. Serve immediately. Makes 4 servings. I am sorry to tell you this, but this dessert has 515 calories per serving. I serve this for very, very special occasions.

COCONUT SALAD STRIPS

Remove crusts from day old bread and cut into 1" strips. Spread with sweetened condensed milk and roll in coconut. Bake at 375 degrees for about 15 minutes or until light brown. Serve as a snack or with a salad.

FRIENDS

Proverbs 18:24 "A man of many companions may come to ruin, but there is a friend who sticks closer than a brother."

As we live our lives and go about our daily routine of work and recreation, I am positive that not one of us is exempt from troubles of one kind or another. It seems there is a constant reminder of the IF right in the middle of l IF e. So often a person asks "If such and such had not happened, or if such should happen?" Just knowing that everyone is included makes the IF go from the over-sized back to normal position in life as it should. One important factor that helps us maintain a calm as we encounter our IFs is to have a good friend.

Orson Wells, the great actor and orator, said that we are most fortunate if we have one person in the world whom we may call our true friend. Sometimes we need to take stock and think about how wonderful it is to have even one steadfast friend. If we have several, we should consider ourselves rich indeed.

In the midst of family activity real friendship is of slow growth. There is rarely friendship at first sight although sometimes the chemistry between two people makes one think there's the basis for such. It is possible that we often mistake friendship and humanity. If a person is ill or in trouble, people will aid and assist him, whereas a person may ignore one in health. The first type of help is only humanity reaching out in time of need. True friendship has its beginning in the heart; it is fed from a hidden source and its springs never run dry. Friendship is love without fanfare. It shelters like the massive branches of a giant magnolia tree. It is stronger than kindred in ever so many ways and is more generous than spring showers. A true friend loves me the way I am. I can think aloud and she understands.

Absence from a friend and then reunion is much like being away from home for a long time and then returning! It's like seeing the flag waving.

It brings a feeling of such exhilaration. Drugs could never dare approach that High.

Faithful friends are hard to find because dear and special friends hold fast to us through trials and triumphs alike. A strong friendship is as rugged and tough as the rope which holds the anchor of the big ship . . . yet should be respected and appreciated as though it were fine crystal.

Good friends are fun! They share giggles at the same time that they demonstrate a loving feeling. A good friend would never say, "Now, I'm telling you this for your own good; you really should lose weight." A good friend does not discuss dieting if she is skinny and you are fat. A friend is one who can't stand the same kind of music you can't stand. The most important quality of a good friend is that the person possesses a good value system and ideals that are respected. Friendship, like all lasting relationships must be based on respect.

Finally, a good friend adds zest to life. As a tribute to friendship, a young son expressed his feelings in this way: "Mama, can you believe it, I like him better than a triple-decker ice cream cone." A good friend is better than vanilla, strawberry and chocolate ice cream even if it is from my favorite ice cream store. I'll have to think though for a minute about pralines 'n cream!

PULL APART BREAKFAST ROLLS

1 pkg. frozen rolls
3/4 c. (firmly packed) brown sugar
1 pkg. butterscotch pudding mix (instant)
1 stick margarine
½ c. chopped nuts (opt.)

Layer frozen rolls in greased tube pan. Sprinkle pudding mix and brown sugar over rolls. Slice margarine over rolls. Sprinkle with nuts. Cover with cloth. Let stand overnight. Bake at 350 degrees for 25-30 minutes. Let stand for 5 minutes. Turn out on serving plate.

This is an especially good treat when there are overnight guests.

FETTUCINI AND SPINACH

1 (8 oz.) pkg. fettucini noodles, cooked and drained
1 (10 oz.) pkg. frozen chopped spinach, thawed and drained
1 clove garlic, finely chopped
¼ c. vegetable oil
1 t. chicken flavor instant bouillon

½ c. water
½ t. basil leaves
1 c. cottage cheese
½ t. salt
¼ c. parmesan cheese
1 T. chopped parsely

In large skillet, cook spinach and garlic in oil 5 minutes, stirring frequently. Dissolve bouillon in water. Add bouillon mixture, basil, cottage cheese and salt to spinach. Stir over low heat until blended. Toss spinach mixture, grated cheese and noodles. Serve in heated dish, garnished with parsley. Refrigerate leftovers.

HELP

Psalm 121:1 "I will lift up my eyes to the hills — where does my help come from? My help comes from the Lord, the Maker of heaven and earth."

The secret word is help. Just plain help. Not, Help? or H E L P! Just help. Like kindness or compassion, help is needed by every living person. No one is as island unto himself. Everybody needs help in one way or another; rich, poor, male and female.

Jesus helped more people in His three short ministering years than the world has room to contain. Sometimes we are tempted to say, when the opportunity comes, "Call on Mrs. So-and-so on the benevolent committee at church," or this source or that foundation. We ought always to accept every challenge and stop belittling ourselves. *We can help.* We can help or we wouldn't have been called on in the first place. *I can help!* We need only to look to the hills from whence cometh *our* help, then pass it on.

It is really a comfort and very rewarding to help someone and know that you've helped. It is a warm feeling to know we are needed.

Let this be a day of helpfulness; be on the lookout for others' needs.

In my own case, if there is not a call asking for my help, there is a blind widow across the street from me who, at any time, welcomes just a simple handshake, (or hug), and a brief or lengthy visit. She has no self-pity but is always cheerful and appreciative of every help no matter what form or shape that help takes. It may be a bowl of soup, a flower, a passing hello or a visit that would allow me to read a little news from the daily paper to her.

Help someone today . . . please.

PARTY TEA PUNCH

2 T. instant tea
½ gallon apple cider
1 qt. orange juice

Put these ingredients in a gallon jug. Add enough water to equal a gallon. Add a cup of sugar. Stir well. Just before serving, fill glasses with crushed ice, a slice of lime and a stemmed maraschino cherry, pour half full of the tea punch and finish filling with ginger ale. Delicious.

HANDCRAFTED

Proverbs 31:13 "She selects wool and flax and works with eager hands."

Fairly often there are people whose paths cross mine, who are such craftsmen that they can look at a toilet tissue core and see a pink satin guest towel holder . . . when all I see is a cardboard cylinder where toilet tissue used to be.

There are times, though, when I decide that if I'm ever going to have a particular item, I'm going to have to make it myself. It would be far better if I could just dismiss it from my mind or, better yet, go ahead and buy it, even if it is overpriced, but beautiful.

It all started when, just recently, I was in our gift shop which is operated by our Associated Women's Organization for Mars Hill Bible School. There were about a half dozen absolutely gorgeous hand-made lace hats. The kind that appear to be of the Victorian period and are used strictly for decoration. I think women hang them on a wall or bed-post or lay them on the bed. I was admiring the hats and saying that I was getting ready to have a bridal luncheon for the daughter of one of our good friends and how pretty one would look in our bedroom, when one of the people who made the hats said, "Why don't you make one for yourself. They are so simple to make, my daughter who is in the 6th grade can make them."

Now, let me inject right here something that is an absolute fact. If someone who is very smart with any kind of handcrafts, be it creating something from toilet tissue cores or sewing a fine seam, says, "It's so simple even a child can do it," the interpretation is, "You'd better leave it alone, it is nearly impossible."

However, I am a slow learner and apparently have a very poor memory, for as she was telling me how simple the hat was to make and how a child can throw a masterpiece together while listening to her latest LP, I had visions of a lacy illusion lying nonchalantly on my bed. I suddenly got an exhilarated feeling of "you can do it" while standing there admiring the hat and listening to her simple instructions.

She said, "You just go to a Wal-Mart or K-Mart and get the doily, dip it in a permanent fixative solution saturating it, and lay it out flat on plastic wrap on a table to dry."

I could hardly wait to get to a store to buy the necessary items for my hat. As soon as I reached home, I started working on the first step of hat making. I followed directions to the letter, except, I forgot to ask what she used for shaping the crown. I thought, "Oh well, surely I can figure that out for myself, I don't need to call her just to ask something that simple."

I reached up in the cabinet and got a cereal bowl (which turned out to be John's). The doily was saturated and ready to be laid out. I hurriedly turned the bowl "bottom up" and stretched my crocheted doily out to form a most beautiful hat.

In my haste, I forgot to put plastic wrap over the cereal bowl. The hat must dry for 24 hours. At the end of the time period, I was so excited about putting the finishing touches on it; the band of ribbon and pretty mauve and blue flowers. I picked up the hat, peeled off the plastic wrap and reached for the bowl.

I could end my story right here . . . but I won't. It was at this point that I said to myself, "Well, there goes John's cereal bowl!" I figured it would have to be John's because he only eats cereal on Sunday morning and I eat cereal every day. Isn't that good logic?

At first, as I started to pull at the bowl, I kind of giggled to myself and thought "you silly goose. You'll have to run a knife blade around it to get it unstuck."

I ran, or at least tried to run a knife blade around the bowl. A hammer and chisel couldn't get between that doily and bowl. At this point I came near calling the person who told me how easy it was to make a hat and ask her if she had ever had this problem. I soon talked myself out of making the phone call because I could not imagine her, first of all, even entertaining the idea of a cereal bowl as a crown of a hat and then, second, I figured she would say, "I told you to use plastic wrap."

Honestly, my hat is pretty. I've got it hanging on a strong nail (hammered into a stud in the wall.) Needless to say, it would not toss nonchalantly anywhere. And if ever cereal is eaten out of the bowl again, it will have to be out of an inverted Victorian white lace (with blue and mauve flowers) hat.

Have I learned my lesson? Probably not. As a matter of fact, my telephone rang this morning. It was a friend calling to ask if I would like to try my hand at stenciling. She said she had just finished doing a border in the two hallways in her house. She laughed and said, "Before you say 'no', let me tell you that I know you can do it. Even our cat can stencil. She (the cat) came in a while ago, stepped into the paint and stenciled a path down the hall . . . beautifully."

I did a quick analysis of children, cats and handcrafts and declined her offer.

And did I (mistakenly) say at the beginning, something about something being over priced? Forgive me, crafts people. After my bridal luncheon I will offer my hat to the first interested buyer: Hat plus cereal bowl for a mere $50.00. That's a real bargain!

SKILLET ONION BISCUITS

½ c. chopped onion
2 T. butter or margarine
8 oz. can country style biscuits

Preheat over to 425 degrees. In 9" oven-proof fry pan (I prefer iron skillet) saute onions in butter until light golden brown. Push onions to edge of pan. Separate biscuits into 10 biscuits, dip each into pan to coat one side with butter. Arrange buttered side up in pan; spoon onions over biscuits. Bake 10-12 minutes until golden brown. Serve warm.

HOT APPLESAUCE DESSERT

Add a handful of raisins to hot sweetened applesauce. Spread over hot croutons. Sprinkle with sugar and cinnamon and chopped nuts. Serve. Very good.

MARMALADE MUFFINS

Place canned biscuits in ungreased muffin tins and press middle with thumb. Put a pat of butter and a spoonful of marmalade in indention and bake 400 degrees for 12-15 minutes.

GRANDPARENTING

Proverbs 17:6 "Children's children are a crown to the aged, and parents are the pride of their children."

Psalm 103:17 "But from everlasting to everlasting the Lord's love is with those who fear him, and his righteousness with their children's children."

People make a lot of useless mistakes during a lifetime. They never seem to learn except maybe through experience. For instance, do you know of anyone who would wake up his second baby just to see him smile? We have to learn on the poor first baby. Thinking about mistakes though, I think one of the very worst mistakes one makes is to go about saying (before the baby comes, of course) that you intend to treat the first grandchild just like any other baby. That's like saying, "I'm going for a little walk and while I'm at it, I'll climb Mt. Everest!" If that first grandchild should ever turn out to be like any other child, this hairbrained statement might be possible. But who could possibly be expected to compare a bundle of angelic loveliness with anything or anybody?

We were standing at the nursery window with our noses pressed against the glass, waiting. Our son had come from the delivery room about thirty minutes before and told us to watch . . . it wouldn't be long now. We saw the nurse come into the nursery from some other room. She had a baby in her hands and somehow I just knew it was ours. She came over and mouthed, "Simpson?" We looked at her and nodded, "Yes". She held up our baby and said, "It's a girl!" At least that's what I thought she said. I couldn't see because of the tears coursing down my cheeks, and my eyes were blurring so that I could only make out the pink blanket they had her lying on. My husband was absolutely no help whatsoever because his eyes were blurred with tears so much that he had to remove his glasses (and he can't see anything without them). We stood there looking. The nurse placed our lovely little bundle on the scales and mouthed at us again, "Do you see what she weighs?"

Still not able to speak, we shook our heads "No." She wrote down on a card, 9 pounds and 4 ounces. Someone standing nearby told us what the card said. About this time our son, the proud father, came out and assured us that mother and baby were fine. "Have you seen her yet? Dad, we think she has your hair, it all stands in different directions. And Mom, Debbie says she has your eyes, they're dark blue."

My heart was swelled so that to this day, I don't know how it kept from bursting. The emotion I felt was too great to ever think of speaking the words, I am a GRANDMOTHER!

Dear God, it seems like yesterday that my husband and I were sharing the same experience and exciting news with other grandparents. The cycle of life is now complete . . . birth, giving birth and finally a little girl who will probably, someday, replace me. I thank you that this beautiful little girl is healthy and her mother survived the labor and birth.

These new parents will need Your guidance, Father. They are young and inexperienced. A baby is Your great gift to a marriage but it will alter their former lifestyle dramatically. May this new mother always love and cherish her child but never forget that she was a wife first. Give the father the tender, compassionate heart he will need to assume more of the duties and responsibilities of raising their little girl. Remind them both that a healthy marriage, like a plant, needs nourishment to grow, and the only way to receive this is through Your tender care.

Teach me to be a good grandmother. When I am tempted to tell them what I did when ours were small, hold me back. May I please learn to hold my advice until I'm asked . . . that is the hardest part, for me, Father. The responsibility for this infant daughter belongs to our son and his wife. They must be free to raise her as they see fit, not according to our generation. But may they always turn to You for the answers. Amen.

Treat her like any other child?! I don't believe I could ever have possibly said that!

CRACKER PECAN PIE

Beat 3 egg whites stiff. Gradually fold in one cup of sugar, 1/4 t. cream of tartar. Add 10 crushed saltine crackers and 1 c. chopped pecans. Mix well.

Bake in buttered 9" pie pan 30 minutes at 325 degrees. (I take a spatula and try to form the egg whites filling to the shape of the pan.)

Let cool completely. Maybe overnight. Top with chocolate whipped topping. (8 oz. whipped topping mixed with 1/4 c. Hershey chocolate syrup.) This makes a really delicious pie.

TOASTED ALMOND TRUFFLES

½ c. undiluted evaporated milk
1 (11 oz.) pkg. milk chocolate morsels
1 t. almond extract
1 c. finely chopped almonds, toasted
¼ c. sugar

Combine evaporated milk and sugar in small heavy-gauge saucepan. Cook over medium heat until mixture comes to a full boil. Boil 3 minutes; stir constantly. Remove from heat. Stir in morsels and almond extract until morsels melt and mixture is smooth. Chill 45 minutes. Shape into 1-inch balls. Roll in almonds. Chill until ready to serve. Makes about 2½ dozen truffles.

DEDICATION

2 Corinthians 8:5 "And this they did, not as we hoped, but first gave their own selves to the Lord."

Oftentimes, I wonder if we forget what it means to be dedicated to a cause. Have we forgotten the real meaning of dedication? Dedication to God and country.

"I pledge allegiance to the flag of the United States of America and to the Republic for which it stands . . ."

It is such a wonderful feeling to stand, place my hand over my heart, look at the flag and say this pledge. I still get goose bumps every time I say it. I hope we haven't forgotten what this pledge means.

We are saying that we promise to obey the country's laws. This includes the local, state and national laws. Laws at school and laws at home, for they are a great part of the laws of the country. We are promising to be ready, always, to defend or be prepared to defend our town, or our nation if the need arises.

It means to keep informed, pay our debts, taxes, serve as jurors and to vote. Every person, young or old, should be proud and so very thankful for every opportunity to say, "I want to serve as a juror," or, "Sure, I plan to vote in the coming election."

There have been a few occasions where I've known of cases where the person did not want to, or refused to pledge his/her allegiance to the flag of our country. I have a friend who is a teacher in a public high school. She has had several students through the years who, because of their religious preference, refused to stay in the classroom while the pledge of allegiance was being said. Isn't it a pity, since apparently they don't feel they owe this country anything, that they cannot go (or be sent) to a country where rights and privileges are not known, and live there?

And consider our Pledge of Allegiance to God. At one time, or another, in most of our lives, we Pledge our Allegiance to God by saying, "I believe that Jesus is the Son of God." In no way does this interfere with our allegiance to our country. When we make this pledge or promise to God, we should be as ready to uphold it as the one to our flag . . . and more so. We must be ready to fulfill the duty that goes with the pledge.

Dedication has a close kinship to determination. In thinking about true dedication and what it means in our relationship to God, try, if you will, to think of these two people and then decide in your own mind which is truly dedicated.

Here is a person who never seems to run down. I feel sure she gets tired just like everybody else, but she doesn't let it show. Her day is filled with activities that could well be classified under "Good Neighbor" or "Making our Town a Better Place to Live." She visits newcomers in the community, always taking a cake, pie or bread as she goes. If a neighbor is to be out of town for a few days, this woman is the first to say, "I'll get your paper and mail in for you and look after the place while you are gone." She visits the sick and does not bore the patient with tales of her own ailments, but tries to be helpful while there. She is careful to write notes to the discouraged and the young people who are away from home for the first time, letting them know they are in her thoughts.

On the other hand, in the same town, is a woman with the same standards of living. She goes about her day in a different manner. She starts her day with coffee, juice and the morning paper. She enjoys the morning TV games shows. These go to about lunch time and then there's the afternoon TV. She sometimes manages to get out in the afternoon to go shopping or take a walk until it is time to start the evening meal.

On Sunday, both these people are at the service and wouldn't think of missing Sunday night or Wednesday night. It is said continually, of both, "She is truly dedicated to the work of the church. This is evident because she never misses a service."

How could I possibly know these women so well? They are me . . . at different stages of my life.

What is dedication? To commit oneself to a particular course of thought or action. It is wonderful that God looks on the heart and not to outward appearances as we do.

PRALINE WALNUTS OR PECANS

1 c. firmly packed brown sugar
½ c. sugar

¼ t. salt
½ c. water
1 t. vanilla
2½ c. walnuts or pecans

Combine brown sugar, sugar, water and salt in a 3 qt. saucepan. Bring slowly to a boil, stirring constantly until sugar dissolves. Cook to firm ball stage, 246 degrees on candy thermometer. Remove from heat. Add vanilla and nuts. Stir until nuts are well coated. Spread onto waxed paper. Separate nuts with two forks. Cool.

ACT YOUR AGE

1 Corinthians 13:11 "When I was a child, I talked like a child, I thought like a child, I reasoned like a child. When I grew up, I put away childish things."

What on earth could have possibly come over me? There I sat, under the dryer at my favorite hairdresser's shop. She had taken down the curls in the back (my hair is very long and I wear it put up) and left them loose so they would quickly finish drying. The hot air was blowing down and this long hair was swishing all about me. It was at this moment that I must have totally (temporarily of course) lost my mind.

I began to prowl through my purse, looking for something (hopefully sweet) to put in my mouth. The only thing I could find was a piece of soft, double bubble gum left there by my 3 year old granddaughter. I popped it in my mouth and began to chew for all I was worth, trying to keep ahead of the sweet. Finally when the sweet was about gone and I was chewing in real earnest, I began reading a magazine article. It was at this point that I must have reverted back to my younger days, because the next thing I knew, I had blown a huge bubble and it burst with the warm air from the dryer and collapsed into several of the long curls flying around in front of my face.

All of a sudden I became the interest point of all the women in the shop. Some of them thought it so hysterically funny they had to throw their dryer hoods back to keep from butting their heads (in curlers) against the hard surface.

All I could think of to say was a line from a commercial we used to see on TV. I looked all around in my predicament and said, "Well, it sure looks as if I'm in a heap of trouble."

My hairdresser was able to get the bubble gum out by using a slick substance normally used to pull hair through a rubber cap for frosting.

Sometimes, I just don't think! I put my jaws in motion before I had my brain in gear. Do you ever do things like that? Probably not. You may say you wouldn't want to even know anyone who was continually getting into embarrassing situations . . . especially grandmothers!

After everybody in the shop had composed themselves and my hairdresser had done her best to rid my curls of the sticky double-bubble, just about everyone there began confessing embarrassing moments. We all have them . . . most of us wouldn't admit them for the world . . . unless the timing is just right such as was this moment in the beauty salon.

Sometimes we allow our souls to slide into situations that we hate to admit and don't know how to get out. Little things go on to be big things and one day we start thinking about it and don't know what to do . . . and sadly . . . many don't do anything. If only we could have the courage to say, "I'm in a heap o' trouble and need help." *There is always forgiveness.* As the song goes, "Pick yourself up, dust yourself off and start all over again."

I am so glad that I have friends who understand me. I am so glad that I have a Saviour who understands me and a Father who will forgive me and love me when I do things that are wrong.

OUR LITTLE GIRL

Psalm 144:12 "Then our sons in their youth will be like well-nurtured plants, and our daughters will be like pillars carved to adorn a place."

Happily ever after . . . generally speaking. Thank goodness, the majority of married people do love, honor and obey their warmhearted impulses to one another.

I saw a cartoon just before Valentine's Day that showed a man in a flower shop buying a bouquet of roses. The caption read, "This is the last time I'm buying her flowers for Valentine's Day. We're getting married next month."

My friend was dressed in his tuxedo and ready to go to the church building in preparation for his daughter's wedding. He got there early. His wife was somewhere in the building with their daughter, helping her with her dress and veil . . . which, once she got it on . . . made her look like a dream walking around. "A dream of an angel", he was thinking.

It was such a short time ago that he was peering at her through a glass window. Stopping all those who even looked as if they were about to pause as they hurried down the corridor.

"This is my daughter!" he would say, as he pointed to the little pink bundle. "Look at those dimples! She looks just like a doll . . . beautiful . . . looks like her mother!"

"This is my baby girl," he said to the first grade teacher. "Take good care of her. She already knows how to write her name and spell at least ten other words. She can say her A B C's and work simple arithmetic problems . . . she's a little whiz . . . you'll see."

"That's my daughter," he beamed, as he watched her walk with pride across that spacious stage, about to receive her degree (with honors) from his own alma mater.

"This is my baby," he said to the wedding photographer as he put his arm around the beautiful bride. The picture of the bride was being taken at the church the month before the wedding, so that it could be sent to the local newspaper.

How could the time have passed so fleetingly. This lovely creature standing before the large audience gathered for this awesome occasion couldn't be twenty-three years old. It seems such a short time ago that his daughter had been chosen to play the part of Goldilocks in the school play.

"Who comes to give this bride away?" Just as he heard these words from the minister, he shook his head slightly, wondering if the words had been said before and were being repeated. Not I! I don't give her away! She's just leaving on her own accord. Unheard of! What man could he possibly give his little girl to? What man could possibly give away his little girl . . . period?

On second thought . . . young man . . . I do give you my daughter. In giving you my daughter, I give you a little girl who can spend money wildly . . . on eyelash curlers, after bath splash-ons in every fragrance imaginable, lipsticks in shades that would even surprise her Maker and collect telephone calls.

I give you a girl who seldom washed a dish. She didn't have to. We had a dishwasher installed at home and she thinks that away from home, dishes are to be thrown into Pitch-In cans or the waiter picks them up. I give you a girl who had to be coaxed to clean her own room. A girl who called us twice in one semester to say that she had lost one of her contact lenses. I give you a girl who loses her car keys, door keys, wallets, library books, and occasionally, her temper.

Dear Lord, give her young man patience, a strong will, a clear head and the ability to hold a job and make enough money to replace all that she loses. Because, you see, she is very much like her mother . . . but . . . oh, so easy to love.

Bliss is not always handy when needed. To me, there are times, they seem to be more in the early years of marriage, when a mere trifle will bring on an argument. Later on, one usually forgets what the fuss was all about. I remember we were still newlyweds, we had both been told by well-meaning, advice-giving friends, "Don't let the sun go down on your wrath." The sun went down and the moon came up and we (or maybe just I) still had our wrath. The moon went down again and the sun was back up when I awoke and sensed that my husband had already gone to work . . . without any sign that he had had breakfast. I really felt rotten. I wished I had said, "I'm sorry," even if I felt the argument wasn't my doing.

Maybe he would call in a little while. Maybe I should just go ahead and call him. No . . . I would wait for his call, but in the meantime I would bake his favorite pie for supper. That would help melt his heart and soothe his feelings and make it easier for us both to get over hurt feelings. Yes, that was it . . . I would get busy making a pie.

Good grief! Then I remembered what the argument was all about! My meringue on the chocolate pie had watered underneath and an unkind remark had been made as to what the substance reminded him of. The very idea! He had his nerve! Make him a pie! Indeed! I decided to wait a few days before I'd think of making much of anything.

Arguments . . . nearly always . . . start over such trifles as the one just mentioned. A young mother, discussing the behavior of her five year old son, was told: "There are about four ways to persuade people to do what you want; one, pay them; two, make them because you are stronger; three, entertain them, play games . . . they laugh with you and they 'go along' because you are a playmate; four, love them, show it, and they love you back . . . they want to do what pleases you. To raise children . . . and to get along with a mate . . . takes all four, but the best results come from a whole lot of number four."

PLANTATION LUNCHEON

(Many times, I plan this for supper as well as for a luncheon)

Make rounds of cornbread. I have small iron skillets to cook my individual rounds of cornbread. I'm sure you could use squares of cornbread as well. But make as many rounds of cornbread as you have guests. When ready to serve top the cornbread with:

Chopped baked ham and chopped baked chicken, mixed together. Top this with asparagus tips; then pour cheese white sauce over all. I use about 3/4 c. chopped ham/chicken for each person.

CHEESE WHITE SAUCE

2 T. butter or oleo
2 T. flour
1 to 2 cups milk
1 c. grated cheddar cheese

Melt butter, add flour and stir until lightly brown. Add milk and cheese and cook until right consistency. Do not cover. Make just before ready to serve. Plan a fresh green salad and your meal is complete. For dessert I usually have a round of cantaloupe served on a dessert plate, filled with either ice cream or sherbet.

ANGEL CORNBREAD

(Nothing is better with fresh vegetables than this cornbread)

1½ c. plain cornmeal
1 pkg. dry yeast
1 T. sugar
1 t. salt
1½ t. baking powder
1 c. plain flour
½ t. soda
2 eggs, beaten
2 c. buttermilk
½ c. oil

Combine dry ingredients. Combine eggs, milk and oil. Mix with dry ingredients. Bake in greased cornstick pans at 450 degrees, 12-15 minutes. Makes 3 dozen cornsticks. (Note: You'll need to bake muffins or skillet cornbread from this recipe a little longer.)

PINA COLADA PIE

2 graham cracker crusts

Pie Filling: Mix together, 1 pint sour cream
1 large can crushed pineapple
2 pkgs. (small) instant coconut cream pie filling

Mix well and put in two graham cracker pie crusts. This pie is so simple and very, very good. You may want to top it with whipped topping.

ROMANS 8:28

Romans 8:28 "And we know that in all things God works for the good of those who love him, who have been called according to his purpose."

Through the years, I have heard Romans 8:28 quoted for just about every purpose under heaven. No matter what the occasion, Romans 8:28 was suited to the situation. Once, when a crisis had just taken place in the life of some of our friends, the minister preached, that very Sunday, about a marriage falling apart and used the scripture Romans 8:28. Somehow, I kept thinking, that scripture just doesn't fit. I looked around and saw friends who had lost a child; there was another couple whose marriage was in trouble; and, of course, the friends I mentioned earlier whose son had been killed by a drunk driver.

As I sat there, I was thinking, "I just don't believe God intended that scripture to fit every situation." Through the weeks and months to follow, I kept thinking about how that scripture is used so much in situations where it doesn't fit. Apparently someone else had been thinking the same thing for this is what I found.

If you can turn . . .

Your Burdens into Blessings,
Your Valleys into Victories,
Your Setbacks into Comebacks,
Your Scars into Stars,
Your Lemons into Lemonade,
Your Problems into Possibilities,
Your Liabilities into Assets,
Your Obstacles into Opportunities,
Your Stress into Strength,
Your Stumbling Blocks into Stepping Stones,
Your Detours into Destiny,
Your Mudholes into Gold Mines,

Your Pains into Gains,

THEN YOU UNDERSTAND ROMANS 8:28!

My thanks to whoever put this together for it is exactly what I've been thinking for years. I believe that Romans 8:28 comes into its full meaning . . . only . . . when we reach the end of a Christian life.

A GOOD FAMILY OR COMPANY MENU

Broiled or Grilled Pork Chops
Scalloped Pineapple
Broccoli Puff
Cranberry Salad
Rolls
Tea/Coffee

SCALLOPED PINEAPPLE

1 c. butter
4 eggs
2 c. sugar
6 slices white bread cut in cubes
1/4 c. milk
1 No. 2 can pineapple tidbits (reserve juice)

Cream butter and sugar. Add beaten eggs, milk (and enough pineapple juice to measure 2/3 c. liquid - adding to milk), bread cubes and pineapple. Put in buttered baking dish (9 x 13). Bake at 350 degrees for one hour.

BROCCOLI PUFF

10 oz. pkg. cut frozen broccoli
1 can cream mushroom soup
1/2 c. shredded sharp cheese
1/4 c. milk
1/4 c. mayonnaise
1 egg, beaten
1/4 c. bread crumbs
1 T. melted butter

Cook broccoli according to pkg. directions, omitting salt called for. Drain thoroughly. Place broccoli in 10" x 6 1/2" baking dish. Combine soup and cheese. Gradually add milk, mayonnaise and egg to soup mixture, stirring until well blended. Pour over broccoli in baking dish. Combine bread crumbs and butter, sprinkle over soup mixture. Bake at 350 degrees for 45 minutes or until crumbs are lightly brown. Serves 6.

CRANBERRY SALAD

I use the sugar-free Jello, using Raspberry flavor. Use one cup of hot water to mix. Then add canned glass jar of orange-cranberry relish to Jello mixture. Add about ½ c. cold water and ½ c. chopped celery. Put in dish to jell. To serve, cut in squares and add a little dab of mayonnaise on top of each serving. Place on leaf of lettuce.

To keep silver tarnish free . . . put a piece of white chalk in your silver chest.

Edible Birthday decor . . . Make a bouquet of lollipops for a centerpiece. Each child can take home a part of the party decor and everybody's happy.

CURIOSITY

Instances of: Genesis 3:6 (Eve); Genesis 18:23-32 (Abraham); Genesis 32:29 (Jacob); Luke 13:23 (Disciples); John 12:9 (Of Jesus to see Lazarus rise from the dead.)

Once, when I was asked to do the devotional for a meeting I was attending, I asked the hostess if my topic could be *Curiosity.* She asked how on earth did I plan to talk about Curiosity and base it on scripture.

You can do most anything and blame it on Eve. Seriously, I believe curiosity to be a marvelous thing. I just wish I didn't have so much of it. There are two meanings to the word curiosity. The first being of keen desire to know more and learn. The other meaning is being unnecessarily inquisitive and meddling into things which do not concern the person doing the meddling. It's the first meaning we must be most interested in and the one that is healthy.

Eve really was a curious woman . . . or . . . she may have been curious because she was a woman. God made us that way, we just must not go overboard with it.

As long as a woman retains her curiosity, she is a most interesting creature. The minute she loses her curiosity, she begins, that very moment, to die, no matter what her age. A curious woman makes a better and more interesting marriage partner. (I read this in a recent survey conducted among 500 men). A curious woman makes a more compatible friend and a more diligent worker no matter what the job is; she's curious enough about it to see it through. It is curiosity that brings a woman out when a meeting of any sort is announced. She just has to be there to know what's going on. If *your* curiosity is sagging, do something about it! As long as your curiosity is active, you will stay young. Years make no difference. I have seen old women at age 30 and very active 75 year olds. It is up to you.

BREAKFAST SPECIAL SANDWICH

Spread wheat bread with the new soft, spreadable cream cheese. Add strawberry jam and sliced bananas, pears or apples. Delicious!

GLORIFIED RICE

1 c. uncooked rice
2 c. cold water
1 T. margarine
1 t. salt
1 apple
Small can crushed pineapple
1/3 c. sugar
1 1/2 c. miniature marshmallows
1 c. whipped topping

Bring to boil, cover and simmer until all water is absorbed. Stir in small can crushed pineapple (juice too), 1/3 c. sugar and 1 1/2 c. miniature marshmallows. Set aside and let cool. Before serving, fold in 1 c. whipped topping and 1 raw apple coarsely chopped. Delicious! P.S. You might want to add a half cup of light raisins.

COMMUNICATING BY LISTENING

Psalm 46:10 "Be still and know that I am God . . ."

It seems that everywhere I've been lately I've heard talks, seen films or read about Communication. The films we saw concerned the high divorce rate in America, and the narrator said that one of the major causes of divorce is lack of communication. This is true! Haven't you said to your husband or wife, "You just don't understand what I mean!"

Why can't we express ourselves so that we can be understood by those closest to us? Perhaps we were not taught to communicate as children . . . just talk.

Sometimes we need to LISTEN. We can learn so much by being silent and just listening. Nature teaches us this lesson. How many roses have you ever heard blooming? Unfolding its lovely petals with loud claps of thunder! The most beautiful golden wheat field that ever ripened for our hungry bodies did so in perfect silence. Do you find the time to listen, really listen, when your mate is telling you about his or her day? Or, when your child tells you what is going on in his world and how he feels about it? Or are you too tired or too busy to listen right now? Before you know it, the child will be a man, then, how ready will he be to communicate with his wife and the world around him?

The basic fact about conversation is this: it is a partnership, not a rivalry. An authority on the subject of communicating said, "Pit the most articulate, best-informed conversationalist against a non-listener, and the result is as if you tried to bounce a ball against a feather pillow. Conversely, subject an ordinary, run-of-the-mill 'dull talker' to the gentle, exploratory probing of a good listener, and he often turns out to have wells of interest and information that nobody has bothered to tap. The good listener, the person who does not regard lively talk as merely an exercise in self-assertion, adds immeasurably to the art of true conversation . . . and to the joy of those around him."

On the lighter side of communicating what we really mean: The other day I was in a sort of backwoods laundromat. On the door a sign read, *Speed Queens for Community Use.* Inside and over the washing machines, there was another sign that read, "Do not Die in Washers or Sit Thereon."

In Sunday School Class a few years ago we were beginning a study on "Mission Work" with emphasis on our own foreign evangelists. We had put a letter on the blackboard for the children to copy, asking for information about the children in their particular country. We had planned to seal and mail them, just as the children had copied them, to each of our families in foreign fields. At the last minute, we decided to read over what our children had written. One child ended his letter with, "Thank you, we are paying for you."

Then there was the couple who had been married for twenty-five years. Everyone thought them to be the ideal couple. They were always at every service of the church and took part in all of the programs.

The truth of the matter was . . . they didn't get along at all. They argued over everything when they were alone. If the house caught fire and one suggested water . . . the other would object.

Their religious convictions kept them from getting a divorce.

One day, when she felt she just couldn't take it another day, she said to her husband, "Let's get on our knees and pray about our situation. Let's pray that the Lord take one of us and then I'll go live with my sister."

Back to the serious side . . . W.C. Handy said, "Life is something like this trumpet, If you don't put something in it, you don't get anything out, and that's the truth." And I agree. Don't just talk . . . communicate!

CHERRY SURPRISE

2 cans cherry pie filling
1 box white cake mix
1½ c. chopped pecans
½ lb. butter, melted

Spread cherry pie filling in greased 13" x 9" baking pan. Sprinkle cake mix over pie filling. Sprinkle nuts over cake mix. Drizzle with melted butter. Bake at 350 degrees for 50-60 minutes. Cut into squares. Serve plain or with whipped topping.

PRUNE-SPICE CAKE

1 (18 ½ oz.) pkg. spice cake mix
1 (3 ¾ oz.) pkg. vanilla instant pudding mix
1 (7 ¾ oz.) jar junior prunes with tapioca
¾ c. water
½ c. cooking oil
4 eggs
1 t. lemon extract

Place mixes in mixing bowl. Add other ingredients and mix 2 minutes. Pour batter into a greased and floured 10 x 4" tube pan. Bake at 325 degrees for 50 to 55 minutes. Cool cake in pan for 30 minutes; remove and add Banana Glaze.

Banana Glaze:

½ med-sized banana
2 c. powdered sugar
1 T. lemon juice

Mash banana and add lemon juice. Gradually add powdered sugar, beating after each addition. Pour and spread on cake.

I CAME TO CUT YOUR GRASS

Matthew 25:40 "The King will reply, 'I tell you the truth, whatever you did for one of the least of these brothers of mine, you did for me.' "

The young mother had just arrived home with her new baby. The four year old "big" sister was running and jumping all over the place, excited about "mommie being home and bringing a new baby." The breakfast dishes were stacked on the counter top, dirty clothes were piled in the floor next to the washing machine and the kitchen garbage pail looked as if it was about to spill its contents, it was so full.

An older woman from the church came by to help welcome the new baby and to say "hello" to the parents and the four year old. She sat down for a few minutes, talked about how different it was these days when babies are born and how it was 40 years ago. "I don't think I'd want my husband in there with me, even if he'd agree to it . . . which he wouldn't."

The new mother was saying that she liked having her husband share the whole experience, after all, he was the other half of the team.

Looking around, taking in the whole scene, the visitor then said, "Well, hurry up and bring that baby to church. You can't get them started any too soon . . . oh . . . and if there is any way we can help you, you just let us know . . . you hear?"

He was in his middle 70's and was recovering from a shoulder injury and an infected hand. A friend dropped in to "see how he was doing." After a thirty minute visit, the friend said, "It's good to see you're able to be up and about. I'm going to have to get on home. I'm going to remember you in my prayers, and if there's anything else I can do, just holler."

The one being visited thanked him for dropping by and said, "After another week or so, I think I'm going to be able to get out of the house a little and maybe cut the grass. I think it's about knee high out there now."

The next day, another of his friends came to check on him and to bring a soothing skin ointment that he thought would help the shoulder when rubbed on. After about five minutes, the friend said, "Look, you get your wife to rub that lotion on tonight and keep taking your antibiotics. You've already been in too long. We miss you when you're out of circulation. You take care of yourself and if you'll behave, you can come out and sit and watch me for a little while . . . 'cause actually, I just came by to cut your grass."

Who do we think we are fooling? We sometimes think that if Christianity can't be paid for by check . . . well . . . we don't think much beyond that.

EASY CARAMEL PECAN BARS

10 oz. can biscuits
1 c. firmly packed brown sugar
1 c. chopped pecans
½ c. butter or margarine, melted
1 t. cinnamon
Pecan halves if desired

Preheat oven to 375 degrees. Separate biscuit dough into 10 biscuits. Separate each biscuit into 2 layers; arrange layers in ungreased 13" x 9" pan. Press over bottom and ½" up sides to form crust. Combine remaining ingredients. Spread evenly over dough. Garnish with pecan halves. Bake 15-20 minutes, or until crust is golden brown. Cool; cut into bars.

SAYING GOODBYE

Proverbs 23:19 "Listen, my son, and be wise, and keep your heart on the right path."

There is such a thing as a happy goodbye. For instance: Once a relative was staying with us while recuperating from a very serious illness. We were so happy to see her health returning and progress being made toward her being able to take care of herself and her husband. It really was a joy to say "goodbye" to her, knowing that she was well enough to go to her own home to resume her life there.

There is also the happy goodbye of which I'm unfamiliar as yet. Several years ago, my mother would say about her many grandchildren, (mostly rowdy little boys after several days visit) "It's good to see them come and better to see them go!"

Another happy goodbye is when you remember meeting an acquaintance several years ago, one you never really were that crazy about in the first place, and saying, "The next time you're in town, be sure to come by and stay a few days with us". . . and he does.

Those goodbyes are happy goodbyes. One can look back and smile with the memory. Even laugh.

A while back we said "goodbye" to our youngest son. He left for South Korea. He was home for two weeks (after graduating from Auburn University and then four months training at Fort Gordon, Ga.), which seemed more like two days, getting ready to go. About six months before our son graduated, his R.O.T.C. Reserve status was changed, without prior notice, from Reserves to Active Duty. So you can imagine what a shock this in itself was, much less four months at Fort Gordon, Ga., then off to South Korea. We laughed and planned and plotted as to what we would want him to buy for us if the price was right. We tried to imagine what life would be like in a culture so foreign to us, always reassuring ourselves with , "They're probably no different once you get to know them."

It was two days . . . and counting . . . before he had to leave. I spent the day washing, ironing, pressing and folding; and telling him to start packing, and reminding him, "he could not wait until the day he had to leave and expect to get packed." I felt like I imagine a mother bird must feel when she has to push her own from the nest.

I cooked his favorite meal that night. The realization of leaving had set in and he couldn't eat.

Day one . . . and counting. Sign car over to Dad's name for selling. Do a dozen errands of things that have to be taken care of for the next year, banking, all bills paid, answer calls from close friends wishing to say goodbye, and starting the hard part; saying goodbye to brother and sister-in-law and five month old niece.

Departure day. He had expressed how wonderful it felt to be sleeping on his own bed, so we let him sleep until 10 a.m. (knowing he had not gone to sleep until very late the night before.) I called to him that he still had a few things to do and must get up. He showered, had early lunch with his best friend and came home to get dressed to leave.

How handsome he looked in his military uniform. My mind took a flying trip back to a day about 40 years ago when my brother was leaving for the Navy. We lived in the country and were country-folks. He was only 17 years old and had not even graduated from high school. He knew he was going to have to go to war so he volunteered for the Navy. On the morning he was to leave, we all said "goodbye," all 10 of us children and Mama. I remember she told him as he was leaving, "Son, don't forget who you are." (This, I realize now, had very little to do with his name, but everything to do with values and principles.)

Mama walked to the main road with my brother where he caught a Greyhound bus into town. There he would board a train to take him to Norfolk, Va. (which seemed to us about as far from home as you could get.)

The morning our son left, I kept thinking of my mother. How she must have felt. And my brother . . . he must have felt fear beyond description.

I wasn't able to tell our son all the things I would like to have said. I would have become too emotional and he would have said, "Now, Mama, don't start that," and would have walked outside. I wrote down all the things I would have said if I could have. I put the letter inside his briefcase, marked, "Open in Korea."

His best friend took him to the airport, for he said (to his dad and me), "I don't want you to go to the airport with me. It's better for me if you stay home."

Korea is about 8,000 miles from Tuscumbia, Alabama. There are so many things for which we are thankful. The most important being, we are at peace with the Koreans. We prayed that our son would remain strong in the faith and hold to good values and self-discipline . . . and remember who he is.

Proverbs 1:8,9 "Listen, my son, to your father's instruction and do not forsake your mother's teaching. They will be a garland to grace your head and a chain to adorn your neck."

ONE OF OUR FAVORITE MENUS

1 Peter 4:9 "Offer hospitality to one another without grumbling."

BARBECUED BURGERS

(This is one of the best recipes that has come our way lately.)

1 c. soft bread crumbs
½ c. milk
1½ lbs. ground chuck
2 T. Worcestershire sauce
2 T. vinegar
2 small onions, sliced
½ t. salt and pepper
¼ c. sugar
1 c. catsup

Mix bread crumbs, milk, ground chuck, salt and pepper; make into 4 large patties. Put in skillet (You may wish to add a little oil). Brown on both sides. Drain off fat. Mix all other ingredients and pour over burgers. Cover and simmer for about 20-25 minutes. Slice onions over burgers and continue cooking for about 5-8 minutes. Serve on plate, spoon a little of the sauce over and several onion rings on each. Delicious!

GRAPES A LA SUISSE

(Try this for a light and refreshing dessert)

½ c. seedless grapes
2 T. sour cream
1-2 t. brown sugar

In small bowl, combine grapes and sour cream. Spoon into serving dish; chill slightly. Just before serving, sprinkle with brown sugar. Truly delicious. (As you can see this is a serving for one. You may increase to as many as you wish.

GERMAN-STYLE GREEN BEANS

2 - 3 slices bacon
3 T. chopped onion
16 oz. can French-style green beans, drained
2 T. vinegar
1 T. sugar

In small skillet, fry bacon until crisp. Drain, reserving about 1 T. bacon drippings in skillet. Add onion, saute until tender. Add green beans, vinegar and sugar. Heat until hot. Crumble crisp bacon over beans before serving. (I like to cook mine a little longer than this . . . I cook for about 15 minutes.) 3 servings.

POTATOES ROMANOFF

1 c. frozen hash browns, thawed
½ t. instant minced onion
1/8 t. salt
dash garlic salt
⅓ c. cottage cheese
3 T. dairy sour cream
3 T. shredded cheddar cheese
Paprika

Heat oven to 350 degrees. Grease 2-cup casserole pan. In a small bowl, combine all ingredients except the cheese and paprika. Mix well, spoon into prepared casserole pan.

Bake at 350 degrees for 25-30 minutes or until hot through and through. Sprinkle with cheese and paprika during last 5 minutes. Makes 2 - 3 servings.

RESPONSIBLE FOR YOURSELF

2 Thessalonians 2:11 "For this reason God sends them a powerful delusion so that they will believe a lie."

It is a very sobering thought to think that a thing is right, then have to admit it is not right. In simple matters we sometimes *know* we are right and there is no question about it! Then it is a real shock to our ego to have to find out, much less admit, we are wrong in our thinking.

I remember, while growing up, having strong and definite ideas about how people felt religiously and politically.

Mama was a very strong Christian and Papa was a very strong Republican. I am being totally honest when I tell you that I absolutely grew up thinking that everybody who was a Christian was also a Republican. It was a real shock to me to find out differently . . . that Christians are also Democrats and vice versa.

You may get a chuckle from my ignorance but isn't this the way our faith comes about most times? We embrace whatever our parents believe . . . right or wrong. Isn't this the same predicament in which millions of people are going to find themselves at the Judgment? Telling God our Father, who created us and the universe, that He is wrong. It can't be that way. Our salvation can't possibly hinge on those simple statements in the Bible. It can't be that way because Mama, Papa, preacher, priest, or someone else told us another way. And they can't be wrong!

It doesn't change our destiny one bit . . . what our fathers and forefathers believed . . . if . . . what they believed is wrong. We are responsible for our own salvation. We must make our calling and election sure. 2 Peter 1:10.

PECAN SWEET POTATO PIE

1½ c. cooked sweet potatoes, mashed
3 eggs, slightly beaten
1 c. evaporated milk
½ c. dark corn syrup
2 T. melted margarine
1 t. salt
1 t. cinnamon
½ t. ginger
½ c. firmly packed brown sugar
1 c. pecans
½ t. nutmeg
1 unbaked 9" pie shell

Beat together sweet potatoes, eggs, milk, syrup, sugar, margarine, salt, and spices. Beat until smooth and frothy. Stir in pecans. Pour into pastry shell. Bake at 425 degrees for 15 minutes. Then reduce temperature to 350 degrees and continue baking for about 45 minutes. Bake until knife blade inserted in center comes out clean.

MEXICAN CHICKEN

2 whole chicken breasts, cooked (about 2½ c. chopped - save broth)
large package Doritos, broken

Sauce:
½ c. chicken broth
½ can Rotel tomatoes
1 can cream of mushroom soup
10 slices American cheese

Line bottom of 13"x 9" dish with Doritos; layer with chopped chicken. Pour sauce over chicken and top with cheese slices. Bake 30 minutes at 350 degrees. Serves 6 to 8.

DUMP CASSEROLE

1 can cream of mushroom soup
1 can chinese noodles (3 oz.)
1 can tuna (6½ oz.) drained
1 lb. can mixed vegetables.

Dump in that order in casserole dish. Bake at 350 degrees until bubbly. About 25 minutes.

NOTE: All recipes appearing in this book have been tested and found to be CHOICE in the Simpson household.

PROBLEMS IN LIFE

Job 5:7 "Yet man is born to trouble as surely as the sparks fly upward."

If all of us could hang our troubles on a clothesline and a great downpour began, everyone would run and grab his own.

All of us have troubles of one kind or another. If you think for one minute that you have more problems than anyone else, you are most certainly mistaken. Recently, it seems, I have heard about more people's problems and troubles than I ever remember having heard before. They are real problems needing some sort of solutions. It makes me hurt inside to hear about deep trouble in someone's life and not be able to say, "Here's what you should do." For most of the time, there doesn't seem to be any solution that is agreeable to the persons involved.

Divorce is still one of the most heart-breaking troubles to come into a family. A few days ago I heard of a couple having just filed for divorce. A family member asked the four year old son of the couple if he understood what the word divorce means. The child said, "It means that either my daddy or my mommie moves away because he/she doesn't want to live with us anymore. But I can't figure out if we don't love each other anymore."

Though these thoughts may not do a thing toward solving any problems, I do not believe we are ever half thankful enough. We must learn to be grateful. I believe that most of life's problems stem from selfishness on someone's part. Someone is not willing to give an inch but is usually ready to grab a yard. This selfishness is not always materialistic, it may be an unforgiving spirit.

We should not take blessings and favors for granted. Generally we have done very little to merit them, so why should we receive them as if they were owed to us. We have been given life and instead of being thankful, many of us go through life murmuring and complaining that we were not born in a different place or at a different time. We complain that we have trials, suffer pain, shed tears and have disappointments. Some even wish they had never been given life at all.

When loving favors are showered on us by friends and loved ones we should receive them with much gratitude because so often these favors have come through some act of self-denial that we may never understand.

We all have burdens. We may think ours is heavier than our neighbor's, but most likely, our neighbor wouldn't agree. We must try not to complain too much about our troubles because the person to whom we confide may be thinking that ours are small by comparison.

Cheerfulness is a great burden-carrier. It will lift you above the everyday trials and annoyances and fill your heart with sunshine. Burdens are a part of our discipline. We can help ourselves and one another if we remember to be cheerful. We can learn to be more thoughtful. A little act of thoughtfulness can delight the sad heart of a friend. And we can learn to be more encouraging to one another. To be generous with our words of encouragement will not impoverish us; it will always prove to enrich us and the one to whom we are talking.

Life's problems will go a little easier for us all if we will try to remember that we were not primarily put on this earth to see through one another, but to see one another through.

LAUGHTER

Psalm 126:2 "Our mouths were filled with laughter, our tongues with songs of joy."

Perhaps this never happened where you attend Bible School and worship services, but it is a tale I recall from growing-up years.

It seems that the preacher was disturbed by the conversation he could see taking place during the song just before the sermon was to begin. He could tolerate it no longer. He decided to try a drastic device to break up the thoughtless practice. He gave directions to the song director to have the audience suddenly hush right in the middle of the chorus. All over the church sped the important information Sister Jones was imparting to Sister Smith: "I fry mine in lard!"

If that little story didn't get a chuckle out of you, maybe we'll settle for a big smile. Laughter is so very important. Doctors tell us that our outlook on life could improve a hundred percent if we would laugh just 30 seconds each hour.

We can use laughter to our own advantage. We can take it with us wherever we go. We can have it in abundance, without cost, and the more we give away the more we keep for ourselves. It is available to us day and night. We shouldn't wait for someone to make us laugh . . . do it yourself. Learn to laugh easily so that the ability is there when you need it.

I am so fortunate to have friends that when we are together, we laugh. There are so many funny things to talk about; however, we don't always have to have things to make us laugh. We just enjoy being together so much that laughter comes naturally. After a day of being together, we all feel so much better and can hardly wait for the next time.

When we are together, it doesn't matter who says what . . . everything is funny. You don't hear a slight chuckle or a dignified "ha, ha, ha." We have real, sure enough belly laughs. The kind that makes you hurt and tears roll down your face.

A recent article said, "When we laugh we contribute to happy living, both ours and others. Treat it as a personalized, individualized Art Form, a cultural pursuit that identifies one as a well-rounded person."

Whenever we feel down we can get a lift with a laugh. Our daily problems can build into stress and strain when unheeded. We can counter them with laughter. "The morale builder that makes our spirit glow with anticipation for a happier day."

I have a brother whose laughter is so infectious that being with him makes you feel good. I feel quite sure that he has things that trouble him every now and then, but rarely does he let it show. People like to be around him, and it would be wonderful if more of us could be the same way, able to laugh . . . even though sometimes we don't feel like laughing. We need laughter. A good sense of humor and the ability to laugh and have a good time are vital to our good health.

All of us have problems. Some of us dwell on them while taking on those of other people. Everyone needs a change of pace once in a while. We can't hide from our problems or run away from the realities of life, but we can hang on to joy. Remind ourselves that we know how to laugh and find the time to have a good time.

Most likely, when your kids grow up, they won't remember the expensive toys and the hundreds of "things" bought for them. The things they'll remember will be the times you had fun together, hiking through the woods, the boys and their dad getting into a toy boat together and seeing who could topple it over first (this was after they had learned to be good swimmers), while the others tried to keep it upright; playing kick the can with the neighborhood kids, then bring them in for hot chocolate and cookies, and many other special times when we laughed together.

I can only go a short time before I feel the need to laugh. These are the times when I feel to the urge to call several of my friends and say "I wish we could get together, I need to laugh." And do you know what? They'll usually respond with, "Let's do . . . I feel like laughing too!"

QUICK AND EASY COOKIE BARS

1 packet crushed graham crackers (about 1½ c. crumbs)
½ c. unsifted all-purpose flour
½ c. melted margarine
2 eggs, beaten
2 c. (12 oz. pkg.) semi-sweet chocolate chips
1 c. chopped nuts (walnuts or pecans)
½ t. baking soda
½ c. firmly packed brown sugar
1 t. vanilla

Thoroughly combine graham cracker crumbs, flour and soda; set aside. Combine melted margarine and brown sugar; stir in eggs, water and vanilla. Gradually add flour mixture; mix well. Stir in 1 cup chocolate chips and nuts. Spread evenly in a greased 13"x 9" pan. Bake at 375 degrees for about 16-18 minutes or until very lightly browned. Remove from oven; immediately sprinkle remaining 1 c. chocolate chips over warm surface. Let stand until chips soften; spread evenly. Cool completely; cut into bars. Makes 24.

LOVE

Hosea 11:4 "I led them with cords of human kindness, with ties of love; I lifted the yoke from their neck and bent down to feed them."

Several days ago, I was sitting in a public place waiting for a friend when I began to really notice the people who passed by. People are truly interesting and can make "waiting time" fly by. It comes as no surprise to say there are all types, shapes and sizes. The one I chose as the most interesting was a very hefty woman with long, platinum hair and a look in her face that said, "I've been around." The thing that really caught my attention was her tattoo. Above her halter top on her left upper arm was a tattoo surrounded by little heart shaped curliques which framed the words, "I am loved."

It is so important to be loved. Most of us would not go to that extent to advertise that we are loved, but it is the most important and greatest emotion in existence. Love is the shortest distance between two hearts or many hearts. It binds us closer together and supplies the loveliest feeling known to the human heart. Loving one another makes us better people and adds more power to our prayers. There is no room for selfishness where there is love. It makes us forgetful of self and thoughtful of others; love helps us bear crosses, carry burdens and endure losses. It leads us to a better way of life and puts us in closer touch with God.

A deep and abiding faith, loyalty and love are absolute musts in a good marriage. The love in a good marriage goes far beyond the first feelings of infatuation during the dating and early marriage period. Love takes time. The love in a good marriage is far more than feelings. Feelings are the least dependable things in the world. To build a marriage on feelings alone would be like building on sand.

When one promises in the wedding ceremony to love, this is not a promise of how one expects to feel. Sometimes . . . many times . . . we feel lousy. After saying "yes" to an encyclopedia salesman with the baby only six months old, knowing full well you can't afford the payments and a husband coming home from work after a day when he was the brunt of the boss's rough morning . . . feeling lousy is really putting it mildly. This is when we can be glad that a marriage is not based on feeling. Feelings come and go, rise and fall . . . we should be so glad that we make no vows about them.

However, we promise to love, comfort, (when his or her day has been rotten), honor (it is a distinct privilege to respect the one with whom we expect to spend the rest of our lives) and keep (to provide with the necessities of life).

There is not a person living who can fully realize the details of the possibilities at the time we make them in faith. And this is where the deep and abiding faith comes in. Marriage is so much more wonderful when we put our Faith first. It was God who said "Cleave to one another" and it is God who can make the cleaving possible. There are so many times when we have to put feelings aside and depend solely on our faith to see us through.

Nothing worthwhile has ever been accomplished through feelings. It takes action. Love is action. Love is courage. Love is determination. Love is sweet and kind and patient and very, very unselfish.

APPLE BUTTER TORTE

Using a box of Honey Graham Crackers, lay three double graham crackers side by side forming a layer 5" x 7½". Spread with apple butter. Add another layer of grahams, then another layer of apple butter. Do this until all crackers are used up.

Frost the torte completely with a large tub of whipped topping including top and sides. Let set in refrigerator over night. This will cut nicely into neat slices. This is very, very good. And oh, so easy to make.

You can also do the same thing using a box of chocolate instant pudding mix. Mix the pudding according to directions and spread between layers of graham crackers.

BARELY SWEET ENGLISH TEA BISCUITS

1½ c. sifted plain flour
¼ c. sugar
½ c. butter (you do need to use real butter)

Sift together flour and sugar into a bowl. Cut in butter until mixture is crumbly, using pastry blender. Mix with hands until dough forms. (The heat from your hands makes the crumbly mixture form into pastry.)

Roll out dough on floured surface to 1/4" thickness. Cut with floured 2 1/2" round cookie cutter. Place 2" apart on ungreased baking sheet. Re-roll dough as needed. Bake 350 degrees for 20 minutes. Makes 12. I always double the recipe.

GOING TO THE DENTIST

Ezekiel 18:2 "What do you people mean by quoting this proverb about the land of Israel: 'The fathers eat sour grapes, and the children's teeth are set on edge'?"

Is there a moment or time in your day or life when you feel that you do your very best thinking? I suppose everyone must have their private time to be creative or to think about their job or home or children. My best time to think has always been while washing dishes. The kitchen is usually completely private (people have a way of vanishing when the table is cleared and the sink is being filled with sudsy water). Another good time to think is while running the vacuum cleaner. One does not have to think about what one is doing while taking care of these routine household tasks. You just do them and think about something else . . . something fun is best . . . the work goes faster that way and sometimes it can even be rushed so that the fun project can become a reality.

Lately, I have been making regular visits to the dentist. It was during the series of trips to his office that I made a startling discovery. That is where I can do my genius thinking! Those trivial run-of-the-mill creative type imaginings are nothing compared to the deep stuff you can come up with in the dentist's chair.

I had no more than taken my designated seat, been bibbed and toweled, and laid back and shot, until something that felt like an automobile jack was put in my mouth. It was pumped up until my jaw bone felt like it had reached the cracking stage. Inside the other jaw, a water hose, suction pump and large balls of cotton were packed in until I could hardly stick my tongue through (in case I wanted to). It was at this point that my startling discovery was made. My dentist stopped what he was doing, came around and stood so that he was looking me in the eye (one was closed because of the jacked-up jaw) and said, "Mrs. Simpson, what is your opinion of the World's Fair?"

It was at this point that I felt the tremendously strong urge to stick my tongue through the bale of cotton. (Not about the World's Fair, but at him for having me at such a disadvantage.)

I must have gotten a sort of glazed look in my eye because he said, "Oh, I'll bet you haven't gone yet, have you?"

By the time I was able to nod my head "yes" he had gone back to his stool, I'm sure, with thoughts of "What question will I ask her next?"

So as to put my mind out and away from what was going on right then around and to me, I started thinking about things like little boys growing up, grandchildren, how people either use their time or waste it, and our boys in the Military. And then I began to think about even harder things . . . things you would probably never know if it were not for people using their private "special thinking times." I thought of things like when you meet someone you like, your eyebrows go up! Now, had you ever thought of that? And here's another one for you, everytime you laugh you burn up three and one-half calories. Isn't that great! Makes you want to have a real belly laugh doesn't it? And how about this? A bat can eat 1,000 insects in just one hour . . . if he wants to. If you should want to argue with that, really, it would be "no contest" because if you should ever know of a bat who ate less, I would just say, "He ate all he cared to . . . but he could have eaten 1,000 if he had wanted to."

Oh, there are so many other things that I thought about "while under the influence" but I will save them for another time. I even had a thought that these important things that came to me so crystal clear should be written in a book for research purposes for future generations. But to my great surprise, a day or so ago, I walked into a book store, picked up a copy of *The Bad Speller's Dictionary* (which I love and am so grateful for) and lo and behold . . . there before my very eyes was a book called, *Things No One Ever Tells You*. I am certain that the author of that book has spent endless hours at his dentist's office!

CHEESE WAFERS

2 sticks oleo
2 c. grated cheese
2 c. flour
2 c. rice crispies

Cream first 3 items, then add slowly to rice crispies. Cook on ungreased cookie sheet 20 minutes at 350 degrees.

(I should say, you form balls about the size of walnuts and flatten out with a fork to bake.)

QUICK SPICED PEACHES

1 lg. can peaches
½ c. white corn syrup
½ c. vinegar
1 T. pickling spices

Add spice and vinegar to syrup. Boil 10 minutes. Add peaches and simmer 5 more minutes. Chill and serve. Serves 6.

THINGS WE ARE NOT TEACHING OUR CHILDREN

Deuteronomy 6:6,7 "These commandments that I give you today are to be upon your hearts. Impress them on your children. Talk about them when you sit at home and when you walk along the road, when you lie down and when you get up."

Recently, I've heard more than one person lamenting the fact that either their child or grandchild, about school age, could not tie a shoe lace.

It seems that now-a-days, children's shoes are either slip-ons, buckle or have Velcro fasteners.

Unless you're a grandmother you might not have encountered this newest bit of technology . . . or a mother with older children as well as a new one.

At first, I, like they, thought "what is this world coming to . . . when children no longer learn to tie shoe laces." The next thing you know, we'll be depriving them of the feeling of "getting a star" for cleaning their plates.

I've taken a little time to think about all this . . . shoe laces (or the lack of them) in particular. I have come to the conclusion that things aren't so bad after all. There are many things that were necessary to learn as I was growing up that were no longer to be learned as we had our children. This phenomenon is known as progress. The most drastic change that comes to my mind is the fact that as I grew up, out in the country, my mother cooked on a wood-burning cook stove. Of course, as our children came along, woodburning cook stoves were things of the past. Perhaps that is not a good comparison to shoe laces, but my point is that with progress comes change . . . and sometimes . . . we balk at change.

I am told that children no longer learn their multiplication tables. Horrors! What do they do when they want to know "what is two-dum 5?" They whip out pocket computers . . . that's what! Here I am still trying to figure out how you can put fifty cents in a machine, push a button for a thirty-cent candy bar and get back change (most of the time).

Back in my day, the teacher had about lost her patience with Hubert Leroy during a multiplication match. She stood over him saying, "Now, Hubert Leroy, see if you can tell me, 'What is two-dum two? What is two-dum three . . . two-dum four?"

After she had drilled him about ten times and he still had not answered . . . even once, she was really put-out. As she stared at him with hands on hips and said "Well?" Hubert Leroy said, "Miz Mack, I don't even know what twodum is!"

Progress brings change. Often times it is hard for us to accept new and different methods of doing things. We, as parents, were horrified when "New Math" came into being. This was the fore-runner of even bigger things . . . computers. Wasn't it absolutely ingenious the way computers were introduced to our children? Toys! It wasn't hard at all for children to learn about computers for they played games with them.

We should just be glad for all the new technology. There are, however, some things that must not change. We, as parents and grandparents, must continue to make sure our children learn God's Word. This is a Commandment, under the Old Law as well as Christ's instructions to us under the new Covenant. If there was but one thing that I could tell my children and your children for their children, it would be this: Be *sure* your children know God and learn to love Him and His Word. If this is not done, then all is lost.

PEACH ROLL

Pastry:
- 1½ c. self-rising flour
- ½ c. shortening
- ½ c. milk

Mix together and knead several times. Melt 1 stick oleo in pan (I use a pyrex dish 12" x 8" x 2"). Set aside. Roll dough in large round. Use 2 cups peaches (or other fruit or berries). If using canned peaches, drain well. Place peaches on pastry and roll like jelly-roll. Cut into slices and place in baking pan or dish. Sprinkle 2 cups sugar over all then pour two cups water over slices. Do not cover. Bake in oven 350 degrees until crust is brown. NOTE: If using canned, sweetened fruit, cut sugar down to 1½ cups. Also, use juice as part of liquid.

COCOA PUFFS

3 egg whites at room temperature
1/8 t. salt
2 T. unsweetened cocoa powder
¼ t. cream of tartar
¼ c. sugar

Preheat oven to 225 degrees. In small bowl beat egg whites, cream of tartar and salt until foamy with electric mixer at medium speed.

Sprinkle sugar, 1 T. at a time, beating constantly after each. Beat until meringue forms soft peaks. Beat 5 minutes longer after adding last of sugar.

Place cocoa in small strainer over meringue; shake gently to sift cocoa over meringue. Fold in until well blended. Line 2 cookie sheets with foil. Drop by teaspoonful 2" apart. Bake 1½ hours. Turn off oven. Let cookies stand in oven for several hours or overnight. Place in single layer in shallow pan, cover (airtight) and store in cool place. Makes 5 dozen.

LOVE FOR OTHERS IS SOMETIMES SPELLED...TIME

John 17:22 "And the glory which thou gavest me I have given them;"

Upon being introduced to a new friend, I asked her if she worked. She looked sheepish and with some embarrassment answered, "No, I'm just a housewife." Inwardly I rebelled. I thought of all the things I knew to be true and things that I had read such as: a housewife is a wife, mother, companion, counselor, cook, dietitian, teacher, laundress, cleaning lady, medical advisor, financial director, and spiritual leader, that's all! When we ask, "Do you work?" we really mean, "Do you have a job outside your home which brings in money?"

Too often the job of being a housewife is thought of as a period of intellectual stagnation. This need not be so. Opportunities for creativity are endless. One needs only to watch and to observe a day in the life of a mother to see how wide her scope of knowledge and understanding must be.

House cleaning can seem as futile as stringing beads on a string without a knot at the end, or it can be a time in which our thoughts can take us to new heights. It is amazing how far a mind can wander from the dustcloth, dishpan, or washing machine.

A woman needs to employ all her abilities to tackle this vocation of homemaking. She needs to be the stabilizing center around which the household revolves.

A woman can hardly be completely effective in her personal life and in the home without having contacts in the community. This is in no way a conflict of interest. It is a fulfillment. This reaching out to others usually comes after the children are in kindergarten and/or in school.

Volunteer work is a service that comes to my mind. Service in hospitals, homes, church and numerous other community projects.

It is about just such a service and just such a housewife that I wish to tell you . . . via a friend.

Recently there was a Motivating Workshop held in a city in a nearby state. A record crowd was in attendance. They were in the large auditorium for the Keynote speaker. He was one of the "Giants" of the brotherhood. . . in demand all over the country. In the introduction, he was referred to as "an eloquent speaker" as well as a "powerful motivator." He got up to speak and you could hear a pin drop. Nobody wanted to miss a word. Everything he said was something to be remembered and quoted if the listener could retain it all. He was powerful! He had people in his audience who were PhD's. There were many graduate students present as well, (of which my friend was one). There were people in attendance from all walks of life. The spotlight was definitely on this "giant of a speaker."

Over in a far corner of this large auditorium, in a dimly lit, sectioned-off area, were about 20 or 30 deaf students from a nearby School for the Deaf. They were soon to be finished with school and would have to go out into the world to make their own way . . . even though deaf. The Administrators of the school had reserved a place at the workshop thinking, "If anybody needed a motivating speech, they did."

Standing before them, in almost darkness so that she wouldn't distract from the speaker, was a young woman about 35-40 years old, interpreting for the deaf. Her fingers were moving at a lightning pace. She was not only interpreting but was also translating some of the more difficult phrases and words into simpler meanings.

My friend said, "As I sat there listening, I began, more and more, to watch the interpreter and even though I could not understand the sign language, I saw how beautiful it was. I also wondered which of the two was the more eloquent and powerful speaker."

"When the speech ended, people stayed in line for 30 minutes or more, just to shake the hand of the well-known speaker. He was told over and over again, how great his message was and how much it meant to them."

"By this time, I had become totally intrigued with the deaf interpreter and so . . . watched what became of her. As soon as the speech ended, she slipped quietly out of the side entrance without the rush of people telling her what a great job she had done. I slipped out the side entrance as well, found her, and told her what a tremendous job she had done and how very beautiful it was."

Very briefly, he learned that she was a housewife and mother. One of her children was deaf and she had gone to classes at night to learn to speak with the sign language. She had done the interpreting that night as a volunteer.

HELPFUL TIP: Add one cup of miniature marshmallows to one-half pint of heavy cream and refrigerate overnight. When you whip the cream, you won't need any sugar, and your yield will be doubled.

ONE OF THOSE TIMES

Ecclesiastes 3:4 "A time to weep and a time to laugh . . . "

Something really delightful happened a few days ago that made me realize that clutzy things don't just happen to me. I have remained embarrassed all of my life just remembering the time when I was about twelve or thirteen years old and was treated to a trip into town from the country. We did not get to go into town very often and I suppose that just the excitement of the trip must have caused me to do what I did. Somehow, I felt that I should carry my umbrella with me even though I remember very well that the sun was shining. On second thought, maybe I just wanted to protect myself from the sun. Anyway, I had my umbrella open as I walked down the streets of Tuscumbia, when I decided to go into the Ten Cent Store. I walked up and down the aisles many times and each time I noticed how friendly the clerks were; they all grinned at me and some even laughed. It was not until I was outside again that I realized I had kept my umbrella over my head all the time I was in the Dime Store.

While visiting a friend a while back, we were driving down a very busy street when I noticed the city's largest hotel with the revolving restaurant on the top floor. I asked my friend if she and her husband had eaten there and she began laughing. After gaining control of herself she explained.

She and her husband, along with another couple decided to go there soon after it opened. They knew it would be expensive but for once in a lifetime, who cared! They were really going to live it up! Nothing but the best! They ordered a dinner that was served in five courses. They very leisurely ate each course, enjoying every bite. Between courses a sip or two of a fruit drink was provided to clear the palate for the next course. As the final morsel of the last course was swallowed, everyone pushed back his/her chair and breathed that long sigh which says, "That was great! I couldn't eat another bite if I had to!"

They knew they had not ordered dessert but just as they were about to call for the check so that they could pay and go, the waiter was there again, this time with a small plate bearing a roll that looked like a chocolate jelly roll of some sort. As soon as she saw the waiter approaching their table, my friend exclaimed, "Oh, I didn't know we were getting dessert! That looks scrumptious."

The men just sort of laid back and watched. As soon as the plates were placed in front of them (I forgot to mention at the beginning that this was one of those restaurants where it is very dark inside) the girls grabbed their forks and tried to dig in . . . only to discover it was a dark brown wet wash cloth for wiping their hands after finishing the meal.

I could identify with her dilemma like you wouldn't believe. It seems that all of my life, there have been hundreds of embarrassing moments or at least more than my share of them.

A few weeks ago I thought for a little while that I had lost my purse. A frantic search was made and finally my purse was found. I was ready to go shopping with a friend who had stopped by for me. She was telling me that her husband had been very careless with his wallet lately. She would find it lying around in the most unlikely places and warned him over and over that one of these days he was going to lose his wallet or it was going to get stolen.

On this particular day when she found his wallet in the front seat of the car with the car unlocked, she made up her mind that she would try to teach him a lesson.

She didn't say anything all evening as he was wondering where he had left his wallet. Finally, as they were about to retire for the night, she told him that before he could get into bed, she needed to see his driver's license and two ID's.

HOW TO MAKE BEEF JERKY

1 (1-2 lb.) flank steak or eye of round
½ c. soy sauce
garlic to taste
lemon pepper to taste

Cut steak with grain in long strips no more than ¼" thick. Combine meat and soy sauce; toss to coat evenly. Drain and discard soy sauce. Sprinkle both sides of strips lightly with seasonings. Place strips in a single layer on an ungreased cookie sheet. Bake at 150 degrees 18-20 hours. (Don't allow temperature to get over 150 degrees.) Partially freeze meat for easier cutting. Store in airtight container.

EASY ROLLS

2 c. biscuit mix
1 stick margarine, softened
8 oz. carton sour cream

Mix all together. Spoon into muffin tins (greased). Makes 14 rolls. These are delicious. Surprise someone you love with a Baker's Dozen plus one tonight. Oh, bake them at about 400 degrees for 20 to 25 minutes.

THAT'S ENTERTAINMENT

1 Peter 4:10 "Each one should use whatever gift he has received to serve others."

One does not live a half century and not learn a few things. The other day one of my friends reminded me of a story we had both read some time back. It seems that "Baroness Rothschild was discussing a party she had given in her weekend chateau. Now that the Ball was over, she had come to a definite conclusion. 'Sixteen hundred people are just too many,' she said."

Now you see, I would have known that. In our weekend house (which also serves us the early part of the week as well) I have occasionally had as many as twenty-six or maybe thirty people and I can't even keep them straight.

The article referring to Baroness Rothschild went on to say, "How would you say goodnight to sixteen hundred people? I suppose over a public address system. And then, after the first thousand left, you could sit and have a quiet cup of coffee with the six hundred that remained. That's always the best part of the evening."

Thinking of Baroness Rothschild reminds me of some of my own methods of entertaining and house keeping. I really don't know why it should, there's not a shred of similarity. It simply supplies a means of getting into my own story.

While the boys were young and underfoot, there was no sense in ever taking the ironing board down. I never got caught up enough to justify trying to find the combination underneath the board to fold it up and then find a place for it. It was much easier just to find a place to put it and leave it there. Some of the boys' things never got ironed . . . they outgrew them before I reached the bottom of the laundry basket. Girls don't know how easy they have it today. Putting freshly washed clothes into the dryer for a few minutes and then being able to fold or hang. Incredible! I really didn't iron all that much if you want to know the truth. I mashed. There are so many tricks you can learn if you just put your mind to it. I learned that I could fold their Buster Browns if they were being put away, then put a hot iron down on the folded shirt and . . . presto . . . it looked like it had been ironed . . . at least a five square inch of it did. And usually the boys grabbed something out of a drawer so fast they didn't notice that the rest of the shirt was a series of folds.

Once when we were having about a dozen people in for dinner, I got busy thinking of the menu, getting groceries and preparing the meal. For our centerpiece, I arranged a large bowl of fresh fruit and placed it on the dining table, warning the boys several times that it would be their scalps if they dared touch the fruit. Finally, one of them said, "Don't worry Mama, at school the other day in our Bible Class, we learned what happened to Adam and Eve after they ate the Centerpiece!"

One day as a friend was watching me try to pitch clothes across the room and into the washing machine (a trick I had learned from one of the boys) she said, "I take it you don't enjoy keeping house."

I asked her what was her first clue. The following rules of housekeeping have been a tremendous boost to me over the years: Windows: Keep at least one window pane clean to check the weather. Once when I didn't do this I sent the kids off with umbrellas for six weeks straight. Dusting: Don't dust the cupboard shelves. Then you can fit things where they belong on the spots where there's no dust. Clean Fixtures: Instead of washing the light fixtures, use stronger bulbs. In three years I've gone from 25 watts to a thousand. In summer, blame the dust on open windows; in winter, on the furnace. If someone points out a cobweb, quickly say, "oh, you mean Sonny's science project. . . " Or . . . you could say . . . "I would have cleaned but I'm helping my son's pediatrician conduct an allergy test."

I love these household hints from Phyllis Diller. They do remind me of the time when I forgot to take down the ironing board before company arrived. (By this time it had become a permanent fixture.) I also forgot to iron the napkins for the table. Our guests were very friendly and lovely so I just sent one of them in to iron the napkins while I finished cooking the bread. Everything worked out just great.

HOLIDAY EGGNOG PUNCH

(This is one of our very favorite things to have at Christmas)

1 gallon whole milk

3 4 oz. pkgs. vanilla instant pudding

3 t. vanilla

1 large and 1 small whipped topping (a 16 oz. and an 8 oz.)
¾ c. sugar

Beat pudding and milk together and add vanilla. Add whipped topping and sugar and beat. Sprinkle with nutmeg. This amount will serve 15 to 20 people. Scrumptious!

FLOWER POWER

Ephesians 4:32 "And be ye kind one to another, tenderhearted, forgiving one another, even as God for Christ's sake doth forgive you."

Several years ago, a young friend who lived a block away would walk the distance to visit anytime he would see me in the yard.

One day, when he had failed to see me for several days, he came calling. In his hand was a beautiful bouquet of pansies. As he handed them to me, he said "Miss Peggy, do you have any candy or any surprises you don't want?"

You can imagine that, of course, I found something for him. However, the story doesn't end there. I knew exactly where the pansies had come from. They were picked (every bloom) from the bed next door. Somehow, I had to explain to the next door neighbor and be thankful to the sweet little friend who felt free to pick the flowers.

My story was so similar to another I read recently.

A piano teacher had a student, whom she said was appropriately named Angela. Quoting the teacher, "She would arrive every Thursday for her lesson with angelic smile and a handful of ruffly flowers. She was so charming that it took me a few weeks before I noticed how the flowers she brought resembled ones blooming down the street. Hoping to avoid problems with a neighbor I didn't know, and trying to plead Angela's case before she got caught with her fingers in the flower bed, I called to explain. After a number of rings, a woman answered.

"Yes, I know about it," she said. "I'm a semi-invalid and spend much of my time looking out my front window. I have often wondered where she took them. I hope they have made you happy. You know, those flowers grow thicker and bloom better if they are picked about once a week and shared with someone."

TRY, TRY AGAIN

Philippians 4:13 "I can do all things through Christ who gives me strength."

God led the children of Israel with a pillar of fire by night and clouds by day. He leads us with glorious promises. We live each day, renewed by His Promises . . . and do our best to fulfill the responsibility that measures up to that reward. We must make a way, with each day, for the opportunities sure to come our way. We must never give in to self-pity and defeat.

I read just the other day of an account which proved to me very vividly the fact that we *never* use all our ability and the fact that we can do *anything* we determine ourselves to do.

It seems that a little girl, visiting her grandmother, was told by her grandmother about a certain rock several hundred feet down from the house on the bank of a little creek. She wanted the rock moved from its place on the creek to the side of the back porch near the steps. The little girl made many trips to look at the rock, always coming back to the grandmother reporting that it was impossible for her, a little seven year old girl, to even move the rock, much less bring it to the house. Each time the grandmother would tell her *she could* and *must* bring the rock to the house. Finally, she told her to only try to move it inch by inch if that was the only way she could maneuver it. After many days the big rock was finally scooted, dragged, rolled and pushed to the side of the porch near the back step. With a tremendous let-go-sigh, the little girl asked, "Grandmother, the rock is here where you wanted it. Now what do you intend to do with it?" "Oh, not a thing, dear," the grandmother said, "I don't even want the rock, but I had you to move it so as to teach you a lesson that you must never forget as long as you live. By moving that impossible rock, you proved that you can do anything you set out to do if you want to do that thing strongly enough." And so it is!

CARAMEL CORN

⅔ cup corn popped in ¼ to ½ c. oil
2 sticks oleo
2 c. brown sugar
½ c. white corn syrup

Mix together, bring to a boil. Take off heat and add 1 t. soda, mix well and pour over corn. Place on cookie sheets and bake in 200 degree oven for 1 hour stirring every 15 minutes. Bet you can't eat just one.

PEACHES FOR FRIED PIES

2 gal. unpeeled, cut-up peaches (you may also do apples the same way)
6-8 c. sugar
2 c. vinegar (apple cider)

Mix and cook until thick (on low heat) or until consistency of peach preserves. (They have to cook a long time.) It should not be too runny or juicy. Put in hot pint jars while boiling hot; seal, or, cool and pack for freezer. When you are ready to make pies, simply make your pastry or use canned biscuits and spoon the amount of peaches you wish to use onto the pastry and seal with fork dipped in water. Bake or fry.

VERY SPECIAL CHILDREN

2 Samuel 4:4 - 9:12,13 "Jonathan son of Saul had a son who was lame in both feet. He was five years old when the news about Saul and Jonathan came from Jezreel. His nurse picked him up and fled, but as she hurried to leave, he fell and became crippled. His name was Mephibosheth . . . and Mephibosheth lived in Jerusalem, because he always ate at the King's table, and he was crippled in both feet."

Today is Stephen's birthday. He is one year old. His parents, grandparents and at least one aunt and uncle will celebrate with him. There will be many others who will be thinking of him and sending him their good wishes.

Stephen is a Down's Syndrome child. When he was born a year ago, all of us thought (maybe with the exception of his mother) that the most traumatic and overwhelming experience that could possibly happen . . . happened!

Stephen's dad was adopted into our family at the age of 13 months through the state's legal adoption channels. When he was in college, he met the girl who was to become his wife. She had been raised in an orphanage in the southern part of the state. It seemed ironic to us that they even met, much less be so drawn to each other that very soon they knew they wanted to spend their lives together.

As soon as my sister and brother-in-law learned that the courtship was serious, they unofficially adopted Deb. She moved into their home, into her own (newly redecorated) bedroom and commuted to school with Sam. From that point on, Sam's folks were Deb's folks and provided her every need . . . clothes, food, school supplies, (tuition, etc.), and love . . . most of all . . . love. When the wedding date was set, Sam's parents were not only the parents of the groom, they became parents of the bride as well.

The wedding was lovely. Several attendants, flowers, reception, music and wedding trip . . . everything any bride could have wished for.

They stayed in school; Sam still taking a full load of about 19 hours a semester while Deb only signed up for a few hours so that she could work part time.

After his studies were completed, Sam graduated from Auburn University with honors. He took a job in Birmingham, at which time Deb enrolled at the University of Alabama, taking a full load of study majoring in Early Childhood training courses.

Upon graduation, she took a job in a department store with a nagging doubt as to "whether or not my education will ever really be a help to me."

They had been married eight years when she learned that she was pregnant. This was truly a time for celebration! Everybody was absolutely elated . . . the grandparents-to-be were ecstatic! The due date was the early part of February.

As the time drew near, I began calling about once a week to ask about Deb and to say, "It's O.K. with us if the baby comes on the 7th", which is our little granddaughter's birthday.

I was told, each time, "We'll call you the minute the baby comes!"

On a Sunday morning . . . early. . . before our alarm clock was due to sound off . . .the telephone rang. My husband answered as I sat up in bed rubbing the sleep from my eyes. He said, "It's Sue!" So that told me that the baby had come; otherwise, she would not be calling so early. I took the phone and excitedly said, "I'll bet you all have a baby!"

There was just enough pause (maybe a second or two) to set off my own alarm system, telling me that something was wrong. I asked, "Sue, is there something wrong?" Silence. Again, "Sue, what's wrong, is there something wrong with Deb? Is the baby here? Is Sam O.K?"

In a voice barely above a whisper I heard her say, "The baby is a boy and he has problems." I asked, "What kind of problems?" Again, silence. I called her name and asked, "Are you still there?"

She was crying so she couldn't answer. I waited. In a minute or so I said, Sue, tell me about the baby. She said, "I can't. I'm hanging up." Quickly, I asked if she was at home or at the hospital. She said, "I'm at home". . . and hung up.

I waited a few minutes to try to think what could possibly have gone wrong. I dialed her number at home. By this time she had composed herself a little and was able to tell me that the baby had been born Saturday night, by C-Section, and the doctor had told them almost immediately that he was 90 percent sure that the baby was a Down's baby.

My sister wasn't at all sure that she even knew what "Down's" meant, but she just knew in her heart that something was terribly wrong. When she asked the doctor, "What is Down's Syndrome?," he explained in brief terms about the baby's chromosomes but also reminded them that there was a 10 percent chance they could be mistaken.

We are inclined to think that they were just about 100 percent sure at the time, but giving a 10 percent doubt gave time for the shock to be absorbed. Three days later, parents and grandparents were told that they were 100 percent sure that Stephen was truly a Down's baby.

For about two weeks, about all we knew to do was cry. It became my sad duty to inform the other members of our family. None of us understood why this had to happen to them. I even made an appointment with my own doctor. I cried again and told him the story, saying that the new parents were the kindest, gentlest, and most patient and sweet couple I had ever known, and with their backgrounds they deserved the very best.

My doctor, who too, is kind and sweet and gentle, said, "You'll just have to try to forget that word 'why' and realize that God put Stephen with parents who would match his own sweet nature, and who are equipped both physically and emotionally to take care of him and teach him with patience and love and understanding." He also said, "You can't possibly understand this now, but in a very short time all of you will realize that he is about the sweetest baby who ever lived, and you'll wonder what your lives would have been without him."

This is absolutely true. Stephen's is a slighter case of Down's and he is very teachable, but that is not the most important thing. The most important thing about him is that he really is the sweetest and most lovable baby; as his doting grandparents say, "Whatever is lacking in Stephen's life is made up a hundred-fold in extra measures of love."

Author's Note:

On the day of Stephen's second birthday, he had to have open heart surgery. He had two holes in his heart and the heart valves had to be reconstructed.

At this time his prognosis is good.

THE RARITY OF GRATITUDE

Psalm 100:4 "Enter his gates with thanksgiving and his courts with praise; give thanks to him and praise his name."

We've all heard the story of the lepers dozens of times. We know it well. Still . . . are we yet to learn from it? I suppose therein lies the problem . . . we hear it but we don't listen.

It's great to do a little something for somebody and have them go on as if you had granted their life's wishes. It would even be greater sometimes if they would simply say, "Thank you." These two simple words seem as difficult to say today as long ago when Jesus wanted so much to hear them from the other nine lepers.

Not long ago, a friend of ours found a pay envelope on the parking lot of his place of employment. It had a very large sum of cash in it. Our friend could identify the owner because the name was on the envelope. A call was made to the owner that it had been found and could be picked up at a particular place that evening. Well, I can imagine how I would feel if my two week's pay had been found and returned after being lost. But I'll have you know that when the lost money was returned to its owner, the owner took it, counted it and then looked at my friend and said, "Looks like it's all here". . . then walked away.

Can you believe it?! Surely that person was grateful. Some people find it impossible to say, "Thank you." Isn't that sad? Sometimes, ingratitude is a result of parents who spoil their children with so many things, the children grow up thinking the world owes them everything and they need not give anything in return . . . not even thanks.

Several weeks ago another incident happened that brought back the memory of the lost money.

Friends of ours went into town to do some shopping. They had a particular need and went to the specialty store that sold that item. They went in and began to look at the item they were thinking about when, after a few minutes, it was obvious to them that they were the only people in the store. They called out to someone, anyone, only to be greeted by silence. After another few minutes the telephone began ringing. They thought that if a clerk was in the back, the ringing of the phone would surely bring him out. However, after a few minutes and many more rings later, no one showed up to answer it. Our friends decided they were completely alone in the store.

Most of the stores surrounding them stayed open until much later. However, they decided that this particular store must have closed earlier except no one locked the door.

They called the Security Officer whose telephone number was listed on the door and told him the circumstances. He asked them to wait there until he arrived.

Upon his arrival, our friends told him that they were only looking at something they hoped someday to be able to buy.

The Security Officer thanked them for notifying him and said, "The owner will be so grateful that he will want to thank you personally. I don't know what item you're looking at, but if it were my store, I'd give it to you."

Our friends replied, "We are happy to have notified you and feel that we were only doing our community duty. If it is O.K., we will go now that you are here."

He thanked them again and told them that he was sure they would hear from the owner soon. He said, "When I think what could have happened, the owner of this store doesn't know how lucky he is!"

I would like to tell you that our friends got a call later that night, or that they were called the next day, or that they received a most gracious note in the mail. I'm sorry to say that it is none of the above. They heard not a word! Isn't that sad.

In Philippians 4:4,6, we have a heavenly promised blessing for a spirit of gratitude. How, then can one learn to be a grateful person? It does have to be learned. When we are born, we are selfish by nature. This is necessary for survival. We have to be taught to be grateful.

When Paul wrote to his beloved fellow Christians at Philippi, he made thankfulness an ingredient of his recipe for the peace of God. He said, ". . . have no anxiety, but in everything make your request known to God in prayer and petition with thanksgiving. The peace of God, which is beyond our utmost understanding, will keep guard over your hearts and your thoughts, in Christ Jesus." Thankfulness certainly seems a commandment with promise here.

In both of his epistles to Christians, Peter begins and ends in an exultation of happiness and well-being which he constantly links with his immense gratitude to God. He exclaims, "Praise be to the God and

Father of our Lord Jesus Christ, who in his great mercy gave us new birth into a living hope by the resurrection of Jesus Christ from the dead." His benediction rings down through the centuries as it comes from a heart so obviously full of thankfulness, "Grace and peace be yours in fullest measure, through the knowledge of God and Jesus our Lord. His divine power has bestowed on us everything that makes for life and true religion . . ."

Jesus, our master example, made thankfulness so much a part of His life that even when He sat on the ground in a place far from dwellings . . . when over a few fish and loaves, jostled by a pressing crowd of people . . . He gave thanks and fed the thousands of hungry ones. Gratitude on the part of Jesus was an intimate part of the mystical and powerful relationship between Him and the Father.

Of Old Testament times, we cannot fail to notice David. How much he must have prayed to have written so many psalms in praise and thanksgiving. He starts his best known poem with a likeness to the Lord as his shepherd, his loving keeper, and concludes that he will surely live with God forever. He received such approval from God as has been expressed toward no other man. For Paul told the Jews of Antioch, that God called David a "man after my own heart." One modern translation says that the grateful psalmist, with some seventy or more immortal pieces of literary thankfulness to his credit, was the kind of man God likes.

But does everyone really have blessings for which to be thankful? Would it help to be handsome and wealthy and the most popular King of Israel? The answer to this is obvious both from the scriptures and from observing people around us today. As for David, because he always maintained an attitude of gratitude does not mean that he was always basking in pleasure on a throne. He spent the best years of his youth on the run, hunted and pursued by the mad King Saul, who knew that David had already been anointed the future king. After he was established in the kingdom, he was plagued by the worst kind of family and household problems. His oldest son ravaged David's lovely daughter. The girl's full brother sought revenge in murder. David and the royal household were driven from Jerusalem for a time by a revolution led by his own son. David's most trusted military leader deliberately disobeyed the king and killed the rebellious son in cold blood.

So it is, all around us today. One of life's paradoxes is that those who seem most happy with their blessings are often the ones who have suffered most.

Gratitude and appreciation for one's blessings seem to come, then, not to those who have the best material surroundings but to those who have *learned* how to master this blessed and peaceful state of thankfulness.

Jesus was on the border between Galilee and Samaria and was met by a band of ten lepers. We know that the Jews had no dealings with the Samaritans; yet in this band there was at least one Samaritan. Here is an example of a great law of life. A common misfortune had broken down the racial and national barriers. In the common tragedy of their leprosy they had forgotten they were Jews and Samaritans and remembered only they were men in need. If a flood surges over a piece of country and the wild animals congregate for safety on some little bit of higher ground, you will find standing peacefully together animals who are natural enemies and who at any other time would do their best to kill each other. Surely, one of the things which should draw all men together is their common need of God.

The lepers stood far off (Leviticus 13:45,45; Numbers 5:2). There was no specified distance at which they should stand, but we know that at least one authority laid it down that, when he was windward of a healthy person, the leper should stand at least fifty yards away. Nothing could better show the utter isolation in which lepers lived.

No story in all the gospels so emotionally shows man's ingratitude. The lepers came to Jesus with desperate longing; He cured them; and nine never came back to give thanks. So often, once a man gets what he wants, he never comes back.

Often we are ungrateful to our parents. There was a time in our lives when a week's neglect would have killed us. Of all living creatures, man requires longest to become able to meet the needs essential for life. There were years when we were dependent on our parents for literally everything. Yet the day often comes when an aged parent becomes a burden; and many young people are unwilling to repay the debt they owe. As King Lear said in the day of his own tragedy:

"How sharper than a serpent's tooth it is to have a thankless child."

Often we are ungrateful to our fellowmen. Few of us have not at some time owed a great deal to someone. Few of us at the moment believed we could ever forget; but few of us in the end satisfy the debt of gratitude we owe. If often happens that a friend, a teacher, a doctor, a surgeon does something for us which is impossible to repay; but the tragedy is that we often do not even try to repay it.

RECIPES WE THINK YOU WILL LIKE

HONEY PEANUT ROLLS

2 T. butter or margarine
2 T. chopped peanuts
2 T. currants
2 T. honey
1/8 t. cinnamon
1 pkg. (6 count) refrigerated biscuits

Combine all ingredients except biscuits in biscuit baking pan. Arrange biscuits on top.

To bake: Bake uncovered in 375 degree oven for 15-18 minutes. Invert on serving platter immediately. Serve warm.

To microwave bake: Micro cook uncovered on 50 percent power (medium) for 3½ to 4 minutes, or until biscuits are done, giving a quarter turn twice. Invert onto serving platter.

STARTER'S STIR-FRY (OR...NEWLYWED MEAL)

1 T. oil
1 med. green pepper, cut into thin strips
½ pound boneless sirloin steak or boneless chicken breasts, cut into thin strips (partially frozen cuts best)
1 can (8 oz.) water chestnuts, drained, sliced
2 envelopes Onion cup-a-soup
2 t. brown sugar
1 t. cornstarch
¼ t. ground ginger
½ cup water
Hot cooked rice

In large skillet or wok, heat oil and cook green pepper one minute. Add beef and cook, stirring frequently, 2 minutes. Add water chestnuts and instant onion soup mix, sugar, cornstarch and ginger blended with water. Cook, stirring frequently, 1 minute or until sauce is thickened. Serve with hot rice. Makes two servings.

Note: you may try adding a package of frozen stir-fry vegetables and perhaps a small can of pineapple chunks, drained.

PECAN CRESCENTS

2 c. all-purpose flour
2 c. chopped pecans

1/4 c. sugar
1 c. melted butter or margarine
2 t. vanilla
powdered sugar

Combine all ingredients except powdered sugar; mix well. Shape dough into crescents. (Dough will be slightly crumbly.) Place on ungreased cookie sheets.

Bake at 325 degrees for 18 to 20 minutes, or until golden. Cool on wire racks and sprinkle with powdered sugar. Makes about 3 dozen.

SOUTHERN SALTED PECANS

1 c. butter
4 c. pecan halves
1 T. salt

Melt butter in a large skillet; add pecans and salt. Stir well to coat; remove from heat. Place pecans in a 13 x 9 baking pan. Bake at 200 degrees for one hour, stirring every 15 minutes. Drain on absorbent paper. 4 cups.

MOTHER

Proverbs 1:8 "Listen, my son, . . . do not forsake your mother's teaching."

The most popular subject in the world is "The Home." Whose heart has not been touched by the singing of "Home, Sweet Home," "Suwannee River," or "My Old Kentucky Home?" During the first World War, the boys sang "Keep the Home Fires Burning," and during the Second World War, "I'm Dreaming of a White Christmas" and "I'll Be Home for Christmas." In poetry, what is finer than Riley's "Out to Old Aunt Mary's" or Edgar A. Guest's "It takes a Heap O' Livin"?

Of the masterpieces in painting, "Whistler's Mother" has been copied millions of times, while "Breaking Home Ties" was the most talked-of-picture at the World's Fair in 1893. In it a country boy is saying "good-bye" to his mother. The trunk is in the wagon and the mother is looking deep into his eyes. She has done all she can do. Will he be an honor to her? Will he render a worthy service?

Exodus 20:12. "Honor your father and your mother, so that you may live long in the land the Lord your God is giving you."

Ephesians 6:1-4. "Children, obey your parents in the Lord, for this is right. Honor your father and mother, which is the first commandment with promise, that it may go well with you and that you may enjoy long life on the earth.

Fathers, do not exasperate your children; instead, bring them up in the training and instruction of the Lord."

Mothers today are no longer little old ladies in lace caps, sitting by the fireplace and old at fifty, as were many of our mothers or grandmothers. They are educated, active, wide-awake women, who dress in the latest fashions, have stylish hairdos, and hold positions of responsibility and trust in many different businesses and professions.

Today, mothers are honored, not merely for the fact of motherhood, for most any woman can become a mother, but because they have been mothers in the real sense of the word. Unfortunately, there are a lot of mothers who are not good.

When is a mother a good mother?

When she provides for her children spiritual as well as physical needs. She looks upon motherhood as a sacred trust, and studies to be a good homemaker. She knows you can't make a dress, build a house, or erect a skyscraper without learning how to do it, and realizes that human life is more important than any of these. So she counts the calories and watches the vitamins that they may have strong bodies. She teaches good attitudes and God's principles from the time the child is born. She wants her children to have a good foundation from which to grow, both spiritually and physically. Ezekiel 16:44. "Everyone who quotes proverbs will quote this proverb about you: 'Like mother, like daughter.' "

She is a companion to the children. She knows it is not enough to cook, sew, and keep the house in order (a servant could do that). Rather, it is the association which she has with the children that turns the house into a home. There she shapes their attitudes and ideals and molds their lives for years to come.

My good friend, Ruby Snell, said, "Pray for your children to be Christians, work at this goal yourself, all else will come."

A good mother shows affection to her family. A lady said one day, "My mother was a good woman, but I cannot remember the time when she ever kissed me or showed any affection." That mother took good care of the body, but denied the child that which meant most to the soul. Mothers, please be generous with your affection.

"A mother's mission in life is not to be a leaning post, but to make leaning unnecessary."

JAM ROLL-UPS

6 slices white bread
½ pkg. (3 oz.) cream cheese, softened
1½ t. jam
⅓ c. sugar
1/8 t. nutmeg
¼ c. margarine, melted

Heat oven to 350 degrees. Trim crusts from bread, mix cream cheese and jam, then spread on bread. Cut each slice into 3 strips. Roll up each strip and secure with a pick. Mix sugar and nutmeg. Dip rolls into margarine, then into sugar-nutmeg mixture. Place on ungreased baking sheet. Bake until crisp, 20-25 minutes.

These are very good as a light dessert or for children who are picky eaters.

HOSPITAL HOSPITALITY

Isaiah 41:6 ". . . each helps the other and says to his brother, 'Be strong!' "

This is for Pink Ladies, Hospital Volunteers and any other service organization with which you may be associated. I am a hospital volunteer. Not too long ago, I was asked by our Director of Volunteers to give a talk at our Awards Banquet. This is that talk. If you are a volunteering person, this is for you.

Just about anything in this world can be bought with money except the warm impulses of the human heart, and they have to be given. They have a priceless power in being able to purchase happiness for two people, the giver and the receiver.

I'm about to tell you of an experience that may prove what I just said to be questionable.

It was my first day on my own as a Pink Lady and my very first errand of the day. Third floor called and asked me to bring a wheel chair to take a patient out; this was Christmas Eve morning. The patient was a young man who obviously was not able to be going home, but his young wife was with him and he was going home on a Hospital Pass. After all, it was Christmas Eve and they had three little ones at home waiting for Santa.

I got to his room with a wheel chair and through excruciating pain, the patient said, "Push the chair up here close to the bed and let me get into it by myself. Don't touch me!"

His wife told me that he had an infection on the bone in his right leg and was just about paralyzed with pain.

After he finally got into the chair, they both warned me, "Don't bump his leg!"

I was scared to death and was as careful as I could be. We got out of the room and down the hall to the elevator where I pushed him in.

My first mistake came when I thought how much better and more enjoyable the ride in the elevator would be if he were facing the door instead of the back wall.

As I was turning him around in the elevator . . . you guessed it . . . I bumped his leg. The poor boy all but fainted and I about had heart failure.

In a moment's time, my hospital career flashed before my eyes. I could just imagine him screaming as we passed the Director's office, "She bumped my leg and it is infected on the bone! I'll probably sue!!!"

I could see the Director, the Hospital Administrator and no telling who else, running out of their offices . . . aghast. . . pointing their fingers at me and saying, "Not everybody is cut out to be a Pink Lady! Let's have your smock, Mrs. Simpson, try to have a good Christmas!"

We got the boy into his car . . . rather, he got himself into his car, saying, "Please don't touch me, I'll manage by myself."

Now, you would think that would be the end of my story, wouldn't you?

About three months after the incident, I was out shopping, visiting a Children's Shop run by one of my good friends. As I walked in I noticed my friend was talking with someone (whom I assumed to be a customer) and immediately, seeing me said, "Peggy, I'd like you to meet my friend, Jane Doe . . . A look of recognition came on Jane's face as she said, "Oh, I know Peggy."

I said, "You do?"

She said, "My husband was in the hospital and you . . ." She didn't have to say another word. I knew who she was, too.

I said, "I'd just as soon not to have bumped into you again . . ." knowing instantly I had used a bad choice of words.

She laughed and said her husband was well now, his leg was fine, and he was back at work.

I'm not sure that that incident on my first day as a Volunteer had anything to do with it but, not too long after that I was trained for the Information Desk. The hospital feels safer with me there.

LEMON-BUTTERED ENGLISH MUFFINS

1/4 c. margarine, softened
1 t. honey
1/2 t. grated lemon peel (I keep the dried peel on hand all the time)
4 - 6 English Muffins, split

In small mixer bowl, beat margarine, honey and lemon peel until well blended and fluffy. Toast muffin halves; spread lemon butter on hot muffins.

COOKING TIP: Better tasting bacon - Dust slices in flour before frying for golden brown, flatter bacon. Grease does not pop while cooking. Even if you Microwave your bacon . . . try this just once and see for yourself what a taste difference.

WOMAN'S WORK

Acts 9:36 "In Joppa there was a disciple named Tabitha (which, when translated, is Dorcas), who was always doing good and helping the poor."

A Chinese man studying the Christian religion once commented: "I read about a man named Jesus Christ who 'went about doing good.' I wonder why I am so easily content with merely 'going about'." As women, we can easily become so bogged down in the endless details of daily living that we feel we're doing well if we just manage to hold our own against dust, dishes, and diapers. Yet most of the outstanding examples of hospitality in the Bible were of women.

Phoebe is remembered to this day because "She hath been a great help to many people, including me," said the writer of Romans (16:2). The Shunammite in 2 Kings 4 was referred to as "A great woman," yet her fame rested in the fact that she had fed the stranger Elisha as he passed by her home and given him a place to spend the night. The godly widow in 1 Timothy 5:10 was described as one having "lodged strangers."

If you own more than one change of clothes, one chair and table, a couple of old blankets, a few staples such as a small bag of flour, some salt, several moldy potatoes and a handful of beans, you have more than a billion of your fellow citizens on this earth. But Christ warned, "To whom much is given, much is required" Luke 12:48b. As women, we have a marvelous opportunity to do good through our homes.

GRACE

Ephesians 2:8 "For it is by grace you have been saved."

A good man died and was at heaven's gate. He was told he would have to have 1000 points to get in. He began a discourse about his good life with, "I was baptized at an early age and have remained faithful throughout all my years." The Gatekeeper nodded and said, "That's good. You now have 1 point."

The good man said, "I married a Christian and we raised several children and they are all faithful Christians." The Gatekeeper said, "That's good. You now have two points."

The man thought very seriously now and said, "I taught a Bible class for 25 years. I served as a Deacon for 15 years, then as an Elder for the rest of my life." The Keeper at heaven's gate said, "Good! That's one point."

Then the man, who by this time was very frightened, said, "by God's loving Grace and Jesus' shed blood, I believe I will be saved."

The Keeper at Heaven's gate said, "Good! That's 1000 points."

—story from Glynn Langston— Cork, Ireland

CARAMEL PIE

One unopened can sweetened condensed milk. Put in large saucepan deep enough to completely submerge in water. Make sure water is over top of can. Bring to low boil then turn to simmer. Simmer (while always making sure can is covered with water—if more water is needed, heat it first, then add) for 2½ hours. Cool. Open and spoon into graham cracker crust. Top with cool whip if desired.

NOTE: When I do this, I always cook at least three cans at a time. They will keep, unopened in the refrigerator until ready for use. This is an excellent way to always be ready with a pie, when needed.

BETTER COMMUNICATIONS WITH FRIENDS, RELATIVES, AND GOD

Psalm 55:12-14 "If any enemy were insulting me, I could endure it; if a foe were raising himself against me, I could hide from him. But it is you, a man like myself, my companion, my close friend, with whom I once enjoyed sweet fellowship as we walked with the throng at the house of God."

This is such a complicated topic, involving the intricate inner-workings of a person's upbringing, surroundings and associates, why should I even want to attempt to write about it?

Because, even with what I just said being true, it is still something we all must do in one way or another. And no matter our age, we can still learn better ways to communicate. It has always been of great interest to me to know some of the reasons why certain people communicate so well while others probably mean to say one thing while implying something entirely different.

Many times I wonder if I really know myself. What makes me do certain things or say things that I shouldn't or need to say something but stay quiet.

Why do certain people exasperate me? Maybe it's because they are smarter than I; or maybe it is a conflict of personalities. It is easy to become irritated by another but very hard sometimes to honestly face the answer.

Why do we react in certain situations? Maybe it is because we are unsure of ourselves or not prepared or resent being caught in that spot.

If we are unwilling to face the answer to our own questions about ourselves, perhaps it is because we are afraid. We are afraid we may have to learn to accept whatever the situation is or we are unwilling to work at changing it if that is what is required.

It is only through finding out what our relationship is in God through

Christ that we learn to value ourselves and become aware of our usefulness to others.

If a Christian woman knows her worth, she is more able to reach out to others. . . accepting them and loving them. This is all of the sometimes painful process of growing up . . . of becoming mature. For most of us the process is slow, but the signs of it are clear and this encourages us.

One of the sure signs of maturity (enabling us to communicate well) is to have a certain emotional elasticity that enables us to enter into a relationship with another person even when we know it could be hazardous. This relationship is known as marriage. Two people putting their entire capacity for joy and pain at the disposal of the other. The reward, which cannot be known in advance, is finding the depth of caring and enjoying and even of suffering.

I have a friend who told me of an experience she and her husband had after several years of marriage that illustrates some of the difficulties of "staying in touch."

Over a period of several months she began noticing and thinking about how little she and her husband ever just really sat down and talked. The more she thought about it the less it seemed they ever had more than a few words in passing.

She began telling him, "Joe, you don't talk to me anymore." He would usually respond with something like, "Hmmmmm" and go on with whatever he was doing. She started letting it stay on her mind more and more and to the point of worrying about it. She would think, "Other couples sit down and have long conversations. They talk about things that go on during the day, on the job, and about the children." But she and Joe only talked in passing or a word here and a word there and maybe if they were lucky, five minutes of dialogue occasionally.

One day, about 9:00 a.m., as Sally was making beds, cleaning off the breakfast table and starting to put a wash in, Joe walked in.

She looked at him in surprise and asked, "What on earth are you doing home?" He had only been gone from home about two hours and it wasn't anywhere near lunch time.

Joe looked at her very sincerely and said, "Sally, could we go to the living room and sit down for a little while. We need to talk."

I don't need to tell you that within the next few instant flashes, she just knew that one of the children had been hurt and the school had called him instead of her and he had come home to break the news; one of them had been kidnapped or killed; or could it be that Joe had lost his job; maybe he had gotten involved with someone else; maybe they were about to lose their house.

Her heart was about to leap out of her chest and she felt faint by the time they walked from the kitchen to the living room . . . all of about 25 seconds.

She sat down and said, "What is it Joe? What is wrong?"

Joe said, "Oh, nothing's wrong, you have been saying for a long time that we don't talk so I asked off for a couple of hours so that we could talk. What did you want to talk about?"

Sally said that she couldn't even have told him the children's names right then, much less come up with a topic of conversation. They sat there looking at each other for a minute or so, then burst out laughing.

Most of us don't always realize that in a good marriage, we do communicate in passing; a word here and a word there. We sometimes know what the other is thinking before even a single word is said. We probably could do without the dramatics such as Sally and Joe experienced; however, perhaps that is what was needed to bring her back to normalcy. She had let her imagination have too much reign. With the dramatization, she was able to realize that she and Joe did talk. We all say things in passing to each other and I'm sure that you will agree that after you've been married for several years, you sort of know what the other is thinking and really don't need to talk all that much. Many times one starts to say something and the other can finish it for him. Isn't that true?

Another quality toward better communications with friends is to be hospitable. Accept people for what they are. We cannot expect to talk, teach, or become friends unless we start with where they are and what they are. To be a friend is to be warm and receptive and sometimes a good listener. *Listening is communicating.* Sometimes we say more with an understanding heart and a listening ear than we would ever be able to say verbally. We don't have to always agree, but at least listen and let the other person know you can be trusted.

Sometimes, that is a difficult quality to achieve . . . to be trustworthy and keep a confidence and be a comforting friend.

During World War II several national magazines carried a poster of a refugee child. The child pictured was torn from her home and everything familiar she had ever known. She was riding in a crowded boxcar to an unknown destination, and was not afraid. She stood beside her mother and held a bit of her mother's skirt in her hand and was comforted through trust.

It goes without saying, the most important form of communication is our communing with God. I don't believe any of us can comprehend the power that lies in our earnest and fervent prayers. Only a very few times have I heard fervent prayers (at least my opinion of what fervent prayer means).

One of those times was when my youngest sister (twenty years old at the time) had a massive cerebral hemorrhage. She had been married only four months. There were many fervent prayers from our own family, but what I will always remember was when we took her to Memphis for a neurosurgeon to diagnose her condition and decide what, if anything, could be done. They went into surgery immediately to remove a mass off her brain. It was during the surgery that one of the Elders from Union Avenue Church of Christ came by, got acquainted with us and heard about my sister's condition. He prayed very fervently with us right then, but he didn't stop there. He called the other elders together, they met at the church building and in turn, each one prayed for her.

To me, that was fervent prayer. As Paul Harvey would say, "Here's the rest of the story." She made almost a complete recovery. She was left with the right side of her peripheral vision impaired and she has never been a really strong person (physically) . . . but . . . she was able to have three sons . . . all grown now.

There were other fervent prayers that I recall. Prayers that I cannot go into for personal and confidential reasons. My husband, who is the best person I have ever known, has prayed earnestly and fervently for our boys . . . and for me.

It absolutely boggles my mind to think how God hears thousands upon thousands of fervent prayers along with ordinary prayers. How grand it is that He can unscramble them all and deal with them in our best interest.

Have you ever thought about the fact that there are prayers, constantly, about everything that is humanly possible to think of? People, throughout the years, have prayed for just about everything in just about every situation.

There are children who pray at night for a baby brother or sister while their mother prays, "not me, Lord, please not me!"

I have heard people in our pulpit at home pray for every missionary we have ever supported, tell God their names and addresses and the different countries in which they have worked.

I have heard one person, on Sunday morning, pray for rain while another, on Sunday night, prayed for continued sunshine so that his crops could be gathered.

We listen to short prayers, long prayers and "I-can-out-do-you" prayers.

We have all endured prayers to impress an audience and been moved by simple prayers that express sincere needs.

I have heard heart-rending prayers that, I am sure, literally shook the gates of heaven.

Prayers come in all sizes and moods and intensities. Prayers vary with every situation.

My husband has prayed many prayers on my behalf. He prayed at the door of the operating room while our first son was being born . . . because both our lives were in deep trouble.

Today, I feel quite sure, there are people praying for thousands of dollars to save a business while others are praying for twenty dollars to buy medicine and food for their children. Some people are praying for a designer dress while others are praying for a pair of shoes. Children are praying for their parents. Parents are praying for their children. And some folks are praying for the same one they've prayed for every day for years. Some people are praying in the midst of a crisis. Some are thanking God for seeing them through a time of deep trouble. Some are rejoicing and some are pleading for relief in their sorrow.

I heard of a child who wanted to pray but had not learned how. He simply said his ABC's to God. When asked what he was doing, by a passing friend noticing his bowed head while calling out the alphabet, the child said, "I don't know how to pray, so I'm telling God my ABC's. He can put it together and spell what I need."

What are you praying for?

CABBAGE CASSEROLE

1 medium cabbage (chopped)
1 medium onion (chopped)
1 can mushroom soup
1 c. bread crumbs
¾ stick oleo
½ lb. Velveeta cheese (cut in chunks)

Boil cabbage in salty water until barely wilted. Saute onion in butter. Add cheese chunks and allow to melt over low heat. Add soup and mix well. Add cabbage and mix well. Add ½ c. bread crumbs seasoned to taste with red pepper and salt. Pour into 3 qt. dish and sprinkle remaining bread crumbs. Bake 20-30 minutes at 350 degrees. Serves 6.

LITTLE THINGS

Luke 17:6 "He replied, 'If you have faith as small as a mustard seed, you can say to this mulberry tree, be uprooted and planted in the sea,' and it will obey you."

A while back I had occasion to hear a man speak who had come to the meeting with impressive credentials. I have no idea if this was the first speech or if he was nervous, but something happened to cause him to start out poorly and then get worse. His speech was a total disaster because he punctuated it with at least four hundred "you know"s. Two little words. I don't believe very many people heard much of anything the man said for listening and only hearing "you know." He may have had important things to say but nobody heard them.

"You know" has become such a common habit among the American people that most who use it in their speech don't realize it. Someone suggested that maybe they replaced "gutter words" in certain people's vocabulary. If this be the case, then it is certainly tolerable, but personally, I don't believe this. Just recently, as I was listening and watching a late night talk show where an actor was being interviewed, his speech was sprinkled thoroughly with "cuss" and "gutter" words . . . all connected with "you know."

Thinking of these two little words and how they can spoil a conversation made me think of how important little things are. It is usually a little thing that we remember most and best. There is a story to the effect that one of the greatest financiers of France got his start by picking up a pin. The boy had applied at a bank for a position, and had been refused. As he was about to leave the room, he saw a pin and stopped to pick it up.

The banker saw the lad pick up the pin and decided that he had the faculty of being careful about detail; so he called him back and gave him the job.

I remember hearing of another incident where a promotion was about to be offered to some deserving young man in a big industrial plant. The three top employees were called in, one at a time, to be interviewed by the Vice President of the company. The young man who was most qualified did not get the promotion. During the course of the interview the Vice President could only see how unkept he looked and that he needed a haircut. The new job called for someone who had pride in himself as well as the position. The job was given to a less qualified man.

This is a lesson everyone should learn. It is so often a fact that the little things are more important, at the time, than the greater things. Most everyone is careful about the big things, but the person of character will look after the little things.

Once there was a young man who applied for a position in a store. He came highly recommended and seemed to have all the qualifications needed. He had occasion to write a letter to the firm, and in that letter he misspelled the word Tuesday. That little error lost him the job. It indicated to the employer that he was not accurate about little things.

(Telling this little story makes me ever so grateful that my husband always proofs whatever I write to make sure I've spelled correctly. I'm a very poor speller.)

Another story I ran across that goes along with this lesson to be learned about taking care of the little things goes like this:

A hired hand who applied for a job on a small farm in the midwest, recounted his experience and qualifications. The farmer hesitated, then said, "I need someone with a sense of responsibility."

"I've always managed to sleep in peace when the wind blows," the man said. He did not explain what he meant, and the farmer did not ask him, but the phrase stuck in his mind . . . he hired the man on a "We'll see-how-things-work-out" basis.

That night the farmer was awakened by a howling storm. Fearful of the damage that might be caused by the high winds, he dressed quickly and went outside. Surprisingly, everything was secure and in order. The barn door was shut with an extra, improvised lock. Double lashings held down tarpaulins over the full hay wagon. There were no tools, no equipment lying around loose for wind and rain to damage. In his shed next to the barn the newly hired man was sleeping soundly. The farmer remembered: "I've always managed to sleep in peace when the wind blows." He knew then what the words meant. He knew he had found, at last, a man with a sense of responsibility.

This little story taken from *Cheer* publication.

People are sometimes influenced more by big events than the little everyday occurrences, but it's the little things in life that are really important.

I was reading something and ran across these facts which point out the importance of little things. I wish to repeat them:

Did you know?. . .

"Termites destroy more property than do earthquakes.

Rodents are more destructive than tornadoes.

More fire losses are caused by matches than by volcanoes.

More sorrow is caused by little words and deeds of unkindness than by open facts of dislike.

More character is damaged by small evils than by flagrant violations of morality."

Not many of us go about doing the big and terrible crimes such as stealing and murdering, but most of our lives are filled with little misdeeds and trifles that can add up and make us miserable. By becoming aware of others and being just a little more thoughtful and a little more honest and a little more caring, we can make the world and ourselves a little better.

MEAT LOAF

1 lb. ground chuck
1 can Van Camp Spanish rice
1 small onion, chopped fine
1/4 lb. ground crackers (saltine)
1/4 c. bell pepper, chopped fine
1 egg, beaten
salt and pepper to taste

Mix well; press into greased loaf pan. Bake 1 1/2 hours at 350 degrees.

SUGAR-FREE APPLE PIE

1 6 oz. can frozen apple juice concentrate
2 T. cornstarch or arrowroot
1 T. margarine
1 t. cinnamon
5 large apples, peeled and sliced
1 recipe for 2-crust pie; can use ready-made crust

Heat juice; thicken with cornstarch or arrowroot. Stir in margarine and cinnamon. Stir in apples carefully. Pour into deep dish pie shell. Cover with other crust. Brush top crust with small amount of melted margarine or milk. Sprinkle with additional cinnamon. Bake 45 minutes at 300 degrees. Serves 10. Great for diabetics. Serving equals 1 bread, 1 fruit and 1 fat.

YOUNG MOTHERS

Proverbs 31:15 "She gets up while it is still dark; she provides food for her family and portions for her servant girls."

Most of the time, we, as the older women, do not realize and have totally forgotten what it is like for mothers of young children. An older woman met a young mother in the local mall one day and asked her, "Why don't you come to our work day at the church building on Thursday morning? You could just put your children in the nursery and plan to spend the morning or day working with us."

That invitation was from someone who had forgotten what it was to "just" get organized to go *anywhere*.

Bottles warmed, diapers, plastic bag, wash cloths, purse, keys, shoes, glasses, sewing basket . . . and on top of all this . . . dealing with keeping the children ready to go . . . once you have them dressed. Sometimes . . . if you have a few minutes to spare . . . this is just enough time for a three year old to find mommie's make-up or the felt-tip markers or a ball point pen and perhaps a dozen other things.

We need to stop and think! Inevitably there will come one day in the future, a time when your purse will be intact as you prepare to leave for anyplace. What's more . . . on that day. . . you'll be able to find both your shoes. But . . . there won't be a little one to ask, every single minute, "Where we goin', Mama? We goin' Bye-Bye?"

As older women, or I should say as an older woman, I would like to remind you that happiness and gentleness in a mama is more to be desired than having "things" just right. A right attitude is more important while you are raising your children than getting involved in many of the "church" programs. Raising your children is the Lord's work. Many of the programs (even the very good ones) can sometimes be termed "church work." There will be time for these later on, for you.

One Sunday, recently, I noticed a young mother's activities as the service ended.

Five Bibles, five Sunday school books, handwork from the toddler class, five coats and caps to collect and put on, two hair ribbons on the floor, pencils to pick up and put in their proper place, and paper to retrieve. All these accompany this young mother into the church pew every Sunday. And all have to be reckoned with as she prepares their exit.

She told me later, that often, her prayer is, "Dear Lord, I know that mothers are supposed to make everyone's life run smoothly. I'm thankful that my husband could worship today as he sat down front to help with Communion. I'm thankful that our children are forming the habit of coming to worship every Sunday. And maybe, this week, I'll have my own quiet time with You during the children's naptime."

My good friend's daughter (who has four children) said, "Seldom do I warm a bottle in the wee hours of the morning but that Proverbs 31:15 comes to mind. 'She gets up while it is still dark and provides food for her family . . . ' I do hope I'll get some rest at night between the time I'm up warming bottles and the time I'll be waiting for them to come in from their dates!"

The same person who said, "Two can live as cheaply as one," said, "Have your children close together." If that person could look in on my young friend with her four children, she would probably say, (as a reminder) "These are the best days of your life". . . which may very well be true, but you have a hard time realizing it right then. Sometimes, if you hear this while you have several children under foot and all of them demanding attention in one way or another, you might wonder what could possibly be ahead for you. As a matter of fact, when I heard this statement one day while I had both children at the crowded doctor's office (mine sick and in danger of catching no telling what else), I asked my informant to repeat the statement several times, since the children were crying in chorus with at least a dozen others in the doctor's over-populated room. Even when I heard her distinctly, it was hard to believe.

God gave me a tremendous and magnificent part of his creation. We had two children . . . boys. It is awesome to think that I was the physical means by which they came to be. It becomes our privilege and responsibility as mothers to teach our children that God is love and they are able to see love in us . . . we become love to our children. Our children are the fruits of our life, thus pointing out our part and place in God's creation. All too soon, the diapers become blue jeans and the stroller becomes a bicycle . . . evolving a short time later into a car. This process usually takes about eighteen years. A long time if you're just beginning, but a brief moment if you've reached the completion of the process. These in-between years become a training ground for how they will act and react in their adulthood. It is so very important to practice hospitality before your children so that they in turn, will be kind and loving and giving in their relationship with others later on.

A LAUGH A DAY

In an age of electronic wizardry and incredible scientific breakthroughs, it is still true that a good daily laugh can help keep sickness at bay.

The well-publicized case of writer Norman Cousins, former editor of Saturday Review, has focused attention on "Humor Therapy." He combated his crippling illness with a prolonged diet of laughter, good humor, and nutritious food.

Cousins, who now lectures at a medical school, describes his laughter regimes as "internal jogging." A funny story, he maintains, causes muscle tension in the listener as he anticipates the punch line. The burst of laughter then speeds up the heart rate, breathing, and circulation, drawing oxygen into the system.

Hearty laughter gives a vigorous workout to abdominal and chest muscles. When laughter subsides, the pulse rate drops below normal and muscles relax. The calming effect can last as long as 45 minutes.

Some recent evidence suggests that laughter actually stimulates release of endorphines, the body's natural pain-killers.

It's not a cure-all, but laughter is a great and inexpensive medicine.

—from *Have a Good Day*— April 1985

THE BIBLE SAYS...OR DOES IT?

2 Timothy 2:15 "Do your best to present yourself to God as one approved, a workman who does not need to be ashamed and who correctly handles the word of truth."

1. The fool doth think he is wise, but the wise man knows himself to be a fool.
2. Open rebuke is better than secret love.
3. A fool and his money are soon parted.
4. Every day is a messenger of God.
5. No man can serve two masters.
6. A merry heart doeth good like a medicine.
7. Cast thy bread upon the waters: For thou shalt find it after many days.
8. It is a wise father that knows his own child.
9. The way to a man's heart is through his stomach.
10. Fair weather cometh out of the north.
11. The good deed drives away the evil deeds.
12. Can two walk together, except they be agreed?
13. Not life, but a good life is to be chiefly valued.
14. There's a divinity that shapes our ends, rough-hew them how we will.
15. I am escaped with the skin of my teeth.
16. Let us eat and drink: For tomorrow we shall die.
17. A continual dripping on a rainy day and a contentious woman are alike.
18. Make haste slowly.
19. We have left undone those things which we ought to have done: And we have done those things which we ought not to have done.

20. Weeping may endure for a night, but joy cometh in the morning.
21. Does thou love life: Then do not squander time, for that is the stuff life is made of.
22. Cowards die many times before their death.
23. Wealth maketh many friends.
24. Rebellion to tyrants is obedience to God.
25. The race is not to the swift, nor the battle to the strong.
26. The fathers have eaten a sour grape, and the children's teeth are set on edge.
27. There is no new thing under the sun.
28. Character is much easier kept than recovered.
29. Man is born unto trouble, as the sparks fly upward.
30. Lost time is never found again.
31. The sleep of a labouring man is sweet.
32. Experience keeps a dear school, but fools will learn in no other.
33. A word to the wise is sufficient.
34. No prophet is accepted in his own country.
35. Be not righteous over much.
36. If wishes were horses, beggars might ride.
37. Better is the end of a thing than the beginning thereof.
38. God helps those who help themselves.
39. Pride goeth before destruction.
40. One picture is worth more than ten thousand words.

Half the quotations are from the Bible. Check the ones you think are Bible quotes. If you got 15 of the 20 Biblical references, you're a Bible student. If you identify the exact source of more than 25 quotations, you are a walking encyclopedia.

Answers on the following page.

KEY TO BIBLE QUIZ

1. Shakespeare, *As You Like It.*
2. Proverbs 27:5
3. Current since 16 century
4. Russian proverb
5. Matthew 6:24
6. Proverbs 17:22
7. Ecclesiastes 11:1
8. Shakespeare, *Merchant of Venice*
9. Current since 19 century
10. Job 37:22
11. The Koran
12. Amos 2:6
13. Plato
14. Shakespeare, *Hamlet*
15. Job 19:20
16. Isaiah 22:13
17. Proverbs 27:15
18. From the Greek
19. Book of Common Prayer
20. Psalm 30:5
21. Ben Franklin, *Poor Richard's Almanac*
22. Shakespeare, *Julius Caesar*
23. Proverbs 19:4

25\. Motto on T. Jefferson's seal

25\. Ecclesiastes 9:11

26\. Jeremiah 31:29 - Ezek. 18:2

27\. Ecclesiastes 1:9

28\. Thomas Paine

29. Job 5:7
30. Ben Franklin
31. Ecclesiastes 5:12
32. Ben Franklin
33. Terence (Roman Dramatist, 50 B.C.)
34. Luke 4:24
35. Ecclesiastes 7:8
36. *John Ray's English Proverbs, 1670*
37. Ecclesiastes 7:8
38. Ben Franklin
39. Proverbs 16:18
40. Chinese Proverb

PUMPKIN CAKE

1 16 oz. can pumpkin
1 13 oz. can evaporated milk
3 eggs, beaten
1 ½ c. sugar
1 t. cinnamon
½ t. nutmeg
½ t. cloves
½ t. ginger
½ t. salt

Mix and pour into 9" x 13" pyrex dish. Sprinkle on top: 1 box yellow cake mix - 1 cup nuts. Pour over: 1 ½ sticks melted butter. Bake one hour at 350 degrees. Last 5 minutes add 1 c. coconut on top. Very good. A great Thanksgiving dessert treat.

GETTING WHAT YOU WANT – WANTING WHAT YOU GET

Joshua 10:9 "Be strong and courageous. Do not be discouraged."
Ecclesiastes 3:1 "There is a time for everything, and a season for every activity under heaven."

There are four categories into which all of our days are divided. Perhaps many of us are not aware of the name of the structure that frames our time but it is there just the same . . . in all our lives. The professional name is *Time Management*. But we, as mothers and homemakers, usually don't call it anything, for most of us stumble upon it completely by accident and really don't even realize it's there. Time Management consists of four parts, they are: *Purpose, Goals, Priorities,* and *Planning*.

In each of our lives, we make decisions and choices every day to determine the management of our time. First, we decide what we want to accomplish . . . these are goals. Then we must establish which are the most important and these are priorities. Then, we must decide how to get them done and this is planning.

Some of us need time for our families; others need time to earn a living. Many women today need time for both. We need time for our parents and time for our friends. We need time for our community and time for ourselves to be creative.

It is those four words we mentioned earlier that will help us get through whatever has to be done. Women who manage to find the time all seem to practice this; they have known their purpose and developed their goals, priorities and plans.

Although she had had only one year of college, a long time ago, her purpose (after becoming a widow) became a college degree in Interior Design. Her source of revenue would soon be gone . . . lasting only until the youngest child reached 18. She was widowed when her four children were in college, high school and junior high. As her two oldest children graduated from college, the third one about to begin and the fourth entering high school, my friend took a part time job working 20-30 hours a week, while enrolled in college taking a full load of study. She managed somehow, to go non-stop, from 7:00 a.m. to 2:00 a.m. for about three years of hard work and study . . . and somehow, in this whirlwind existence, became close friend and confidant to more people than you would believe. By trusting in the Lord, while at the same time giving single-minded attention to her priorities and plans, she graduated magna cum laude at age 48. Today, a full life beckons her from many directions. Besides the many directions her life is taking, she still finds the time to be helpful to her many friends; helping them choose the right fabric, color and/or furnishings they may be shopping for. She has helped many just to re-arrange what they already have to become much more attractive.

The same principles have helped countless other women to do the impossible.

Hopefully you see the lesson here. People never seem to have the same talents, yet, in so many different ways, are kind and helpful to others.

"She layeth her hands to the spindle, and her hands hold the distaff." Proverbs 31:19

There must be something inherent in women that makes them unable to be at rest around unused portions of anything! Whether it is dried flowers, a half cup of brown sugar, half a yard of bright yellow sailcloth; any unused portion brings forth the creative gleam in her eye.

Creativity in the physical and material realm is indeed an art. Ingredients stirred and blended . . . and a cake or casserole cools on the top of the stove. Leaves, fruits and berries . . . and the mantle piece is adorned for the Christmas holiday season.

Do we ever stop to consider the spiritual creativity? The things of the spirit all about us need the creative genius of the woman. Kindness can be lent to the neighbor who feels inadequate; encouragement in a continuous supply, given when that young beautiful mother has given birth to a son and the doctor comes five minutes later and tells them, "Your son has Down's Syndrome"; laughter in the time of despair and the magic of praise can be shared with our own family at the breakfast table when someone has received a high mark on a test paper or received some honor or has just been thoughtful to other members of the family . . . before they leave for school or work.

Teaching and training our children to love the Lord must be our purpose, goal, priority and plan while they are under our care. What they become later in life is their responsibility, but we will be held responsible for their spiritual training while they are young.

Taking a bad situation and making a better one from it shows more skill and deep creativity than the deft, agile fingers of the artist.

Most of our lives are, by necessity, divided between the Mary-things and the Martha-things. I feel sure that most of you do dozens of things every day that God looks on as hospitable. Being kind to your children's friends does not go unnoticed. I was reminded recently that often times children are in need of our sympathy, yet, we rarely think of them when there's a death in the family.

Here is a poem, written by a friend, expressing this need. She lost her father during the Second World War, not from the enemy's fire but from contracting tuberculosis. Here are the last two stanzas of her poem:

> Some cheated death
> on the battle field
> Behind the doors
> Where racking cough was heard.
>
> O, my father, in fevered fantasy
> you felt a mother's tears
> Upon your face.
>
> Did you know . . . when a small hand
> Brushed your cheek in farewell?
> My small world shattered. . .
> And no one heard it.
>
> —Courtney Romer—

When I was a child, I awoke in the mornings with a sense of adventure. I'm still that way today. I cannot sleep late . . . there's always that feeling that I'll miss something if I don't get up. I could never bear to sleep and not see my husband off to work each morning. He's not a big breakfast eater but he does enjoy a sweet roll, orange juice and a cup of hot chocolate. If I did not get up, he would go to work without eating. A little later, I have my cereal and fruit; I just have coffee with him. But getting up early just starts the day off right. I feel so much better. Anything could happen! Before the day is done, I might get a letter; or an envelope filled with cents-off coupons; or I might walk outside and discover the first crocus of the new spring. While I slept, the frost might have left a curtain of lace on the kitchen window which the sun would surely melt if I slept late.

As a child, no amount of routine tasks, such as gathering eggs or filling the always-empty woodbox, could dim the bright edge of adventure that circled my days.

The rolling store came around about once a month (an adventure from my childhood). The one that came to our house was driven and operated by Mr. George Hunter (now deceased). He related this story to me many years after it had happened but I remember it taking place.

On his Rolling Store he had the wonderful *candy apples on a stick*. They were priced at 5 cents each. On this particular day, I ran out and asked for one of the apples. He asked if I had a nickel. I answered, "No sir" but went ahead and got the apple and started licking on it immediately. He then asked if my Mama would give me the nickel for the apple. I was licking as fast as I could and said, "I hope so." Mr. Hunter then said, "Do you think you'll get a spanking?"

I said, "Yes Sir, but it'll be worth it."

So many childish traits must be outgrown. But this sense of adventure should be taken out and dusted and put to daily use. With a heavy schedule of daily work the housewife, or the career woman, may lose her childhood sense of adventure. But she must not lose the fine glow of wonder. The hours can be added together to equal boredom or fulfillment, depending on the individual outlook.

STRAWBERRY BARS

3/4 c. butter or margarine, softened
2 egg yolks
1 t. vanilla
2 c. self-rising flour
1 c. sugar
1 c. pecans, chopped
1/2 c. strawberry jam

Cream butter; gradually add sugar, beating until light and fluffy. Add egg yolks and vanilla, beating well. Gradually stir in flour and pecans.

Pat half of dough evenly in a greased 9-inch square baking pan. Spread strawberry jam evenly over dough in pan. Drop remaining dough by tablespoonfuls over jam; spread evenly. Bake at 325 for 1 hour. Cool. Cut into bars. About 2 dozen.

MAMA

On January 29, 1972, there was an obituary in the local paper that read, Ola Campbell Jeffreys passed away today.

When I'm looking at the paper sometimes I glance over the obituaries just to see if there is anyone's death I might know. I feel as if other people do the same. It doesn't seem natural that one would read obituaries for any other purpose.

But this was Mama. The article went on to say that she was survived by eight daughters and two sons (one son had died in an automobile crash in December of 1941), and that she was 78 years old.

There was no way anyone could know from reading the obituary that she happily awaited death. She did the very best she could with what she had, and this is all the Lord expects of any one. The paper did not say that Ola Campbell Jeffreys died in the Lord. . . but she did.

I remember, at the time, thinking that her death announcement should have made headlines across the nation. It would if everyone could have known Mama.

In her adolescence she was recognized as one of the prettiest girls in the county. Perhaps this was partially due to the fact that she was the great granddaughter of a beautiful Indian Princess. She was petite in stature . . . four feet and ten inches tall and usually weighed slightly over one hundred pounds. She married at the age of sixteen, and at the age of eighteen she had a baby girl. This, in itself, is nothing spectacular; girls do this every day. What made her life extraordinary is this: She was to have a baby from that day of her young life until she was forty-five years old. For twenty-seven years she had a tiny baby to hold and care for, because she had eleven children.

She never seemed unhappy in her situation as well as we can remember. At least, if she was, she didn't tell us. I am the next to the youngest of the children. We all learned, at early ages, what patience meant, and long-suffering and gentleness. She was never a really strong person, physically, yet she worked so hard all of her life. It seems that having a young baby all of the time would have been enough to have kept her in the house (and it should have), but we lived in the country on a farm. She saw to it that we had large vegetable gardens besides the many acres of cotton, corn and whatever else was grown in the fields. It was up to her to lead the way in showing us how to work. Many, many times, after she had children old enough to care for the younger ones, she would work in the fields every morning, come in to cook in the middle of the day, then go back to the fields in the afternoon. Whichever of the older girls would be looking after the baby, would take it to mama at feeding time.

At night, after everyone else had gone to bed, mama would stay up until late (at this time perhaps 10:00 p.m. because in those days, farmers went to bed right after dark) working on quilts or making clothes. I should say that this was fall work. At night in summer, she would stay up, with the help of the older girls, canning fruits and vegetables.

She always said that winter was a welcomed sight and time of year. Looking back, it is not hard to understand why.

Whatever she cooked, she saw to everyone else's needs first, then she ate what was left. It seems strange that we never noticed that until we all grew up. All of my life, at home, I honestly thought the neck of the chicken was her favorite piece . . . never did I realize she ate it because it was the only thing left.

It is interesting now to think about the very large amounts she had to cook. I suppose what I remember most were her blackberry pies (or any pie for that matter). She cooked them in a large tin pan (which we would now know as a dish pan).

How many dozens of nights she must have spent worrying over a sick child. She suffered several years with asthma while two of her children had attacks of the same affliction . . . finally outgrowing it at about five years of age. I think of how many times she must have prayed through cases of Red measles, German measles, mumps, whooping cough, chicken-pox, scarlet fever and even diphtheria . . . vaccines were unheard of. Can you imagine what it must be like to go through all of these diseases eleven times?

In summer months, without fail, the well would go dry. She and the older children would have to take the wash, once or twice a week, to a spring located about 2 miles from our house. The wash pot would also be carried and left there the duration of the dry spell. The clothes would have to be boiled . . . white and colored clothes separately of course. Then washed and rinsed and literally tugged and dragged in tubs back to the house to be hung on the clothes lines.

When she was forty-four years old and her last child was two, her second child (a son) was killed in a car accident in town, about 10 miles from our home. I shall never forget someone, in trying to comfort her, said, "But, Ola, you have ten other children."

Mama said, "Never can one child take another's place in the heart of a mother." Oh, how his death did grieve her.

When she was fifty-four her health began to fail. She began having convulsions. The neurosurgeon in Memphis, Tennessee diagnosed her ailment as brain deterioration caused by a fall she had many years before. A car side-swiped the wagon in which she was riding and the driver of the car never even stopped. Mama fell from the wagon seat while holding a baby in her arms, taking all of the fall while protecting the child.

She was a semi-invalid for about twelve years, then a complete invalid for about eight years.

At first when the doctor told us that her mind would go, we thought we just could not bear to see mama in such a condition. Much later, we came to realize that this was somewhat of a blessing.

In addition to having and caring for eleven children, some of her young years she had her mother-in-law to care for. Our grandmother was in bad health and not able to help with any of the work, but lived with us and was cared for about ten years. Mama never complained so far as we can remember . . . but . . . we do remember one thing she said over and over, "I hope the Lord never lets me live long enough that I become a burden to my children."

If mama had been in her right mind while she was ill those fifteen or sixteen years, she would have thought she was a burden. She was not.

I am so greatful that Ola Campbell Jeffreys lived. I am also very thankful that God gave us the privilege of repaying a small portion of the years and years of care she gave us. How richly God blessed us to have given us such a mother as she. "Who can find a virtuous woman?" We did.

I am now a grandmother. Recently my granddaughter asked me, "Mimi, did Santa give you what you asked for?" This is what I told her, which she surely did not understand at three and three-fourths years old, but perhaps she will read this someday and understand. I said, "Jennifer, darling, I think that instead of us starting to ask for certain things as children do now, we would wait for mama to hint at what we could expect and *that* is what we would want. For instance, a couple of weeks before Christmas, mama would say, "Peggy, maybe Santa will bring you a new doll. One that opens and closes her eyes. Wouldn't that be nice?"

At that moment, a new doll is what I would want more than anything.

Mama would never have hinted at something unless she was sure we would get it. I was very fortunate to have been among the last of the children, for times were a little better and we would get a new toy for Christmas every year.

Bits of Wisdom from Mama

"If your children get on your nerves, treat them as if they were someone else's."

When asked if she was partial to any one of her children, she would answer, "Yes, the one who is sick until he gets well or the one who is out until he comes in."

As our youngest brother left for the Navy during World War II: "Son, don't forget who you are." This had nothing to do with his name but everything to do with his principles.

On letter writing: "Write to your own children as if they were your good friend and to someone else's child as if he were your own."

CONVERSATION

Colossians 4:6 "Let your conversation be always full of grace, seasoned with salt, so that you may know how to answer everyone."

The basic fact about conversation is this: it is a partnership, not a rivalry. Pit the most articulate, best-informed conversationalist against a non-listener, and the result is as if you tried to bounce a ball against a feather pillow. Conversely, subject an ordinary, run-of-the-mill "dull talker" to the gentle, exploratory probing of a good listener, and he often turns out to have wells of interest and information that nobody has bothered to tap. The good listener, the person who does not regard lively talk as merely an exercise in self-assertion, adds immeasurably to the art of true conversation . . . and to the enjoyment of those around him.

—James Nathan Miller—

HAM AND BREAD

1 can (12 oz.) ham or Spam luncheon meat
1 box (8½ oz.) corn muffin mix or make your own
1 can (8 oz.) whole kernel corn, drained
½ c. cheddar cheese, shredded

Cut ham or Spam into 8 slices, then diagonally into 16 triangles. Arrange 8 triangles, spoke fashion, in bottom of a greased 9" pan or skillet. Prepare corn bread mix as directed (or make your own style of cornbread), stir in corn and cheese. Pour into pan. Arrange remaining 8 triangles of meat on top of batter spoke fashion. Bake 30-40 minutes at 400 degrees until cornbread is golden brown. Serve in wedges.

CHICKEN WITH CORNBREAD DRESSING

Chopped onions and celery to taste
1 package Pepperidge Farm stuffing mix
Sage to taste
Chicken Broth
Chicken, cooked, cut into pieces
1 can cream of chicken soup
1 small can evaporated milk

Saute onions and celery in skillet. Add to stuffing mix in large bowl. Add sage; mix well. Add enough chicken broth for desired consistency. Place chicken in bottom of casserole. Mix soup and milk; pour over chicken. Cover with stuffing mixture. Bake at 350 degrees for 30 minutes.

This is a good holiday meal. Along with the chicken and dressing, you might want to serve *Magic Muffins, Sweet Potato Casserole,* a *Broccoli* casserole and *Nutty Bananas* (a side dish).

MAGIC MUFFINS

4 c. biscuit mix
1/2 c. sugar
1/4 c. melted margarine
2 eggs, beaten
1 1/2 c. milk

Combine all ingredients in medium mixing bowl, stirring just until moistened. Spoon batter into greased muffin pans, filling 2/3 full. Bake at 400 for 15-20 minutes. 20 muffins.

NUTTY BANANAS

1 c. mayonnaise or salad dressing
1/4 c. milk
2-3 T. sugar
6 bananas
2 c. salted blanched peanuts, chopped fine
maraschino cherries (optional)

Combine mayonnaise, milk and sugar. Mix well. Slice 2 bananas and place in 2 qt. casserole. Spread 1/2 of mayonnaise mixture evenly over bananas; sprinkle with 1/3 of ground peanuts. Repeat layers twice. Garnish with chopped maraschino cherries if desired. This dish may be assembled 1 hour before serving and refrigerated. 6 - 8 servings.

CHOCOLATE MELTAWAYS

¾ c. butter or margarine, softened
1 c. sugar
1 egg
2 (1-oz) envelopes liquid baking chocolate
2 T. milk
1 t. vanilla
2 c. all-purpose flour
¼ t. salt
½ c. chocolate drink mix
½ c. chopped pecans

Cream butter; gradually add sugar, beating until light and fluffy. Add next 4 ingredients, and beat well.

Combine flour and salt; gradually add to creamed mixture, beating just until smooth. Chill dough 1 to 2 hours.

Combine drink mix and pecans. Shape dough into ¾-inch balls; roll in pecan mixture. Place on ungreased cookie sheets. Bake at 350 degrees for 10 minutes. Cool on wire racks. Makes about 6½ dozen.

LEARN TO BE GRATEFUL

1 Thessalonians 5:18 "In everything give thanks; for this is the will of God in Christ Jesus concerning you."

Learn to be grateful; don't take blessings and favors for granted. We owe God everything. What can we do for Him? To begin with, He has given us our lives. Instead of being grateful for each new day, we murmur and complain that He has not done more for us. We must have trials, we must suffer pain, we must shed tears and bear sorrow and have disappointments and lose friends . . . but oh, ingratitude! How we must grieve Him with our moanings.

So many of us never learn how to live. Be glad you are alive. Make yourself a gift for God; look up and be thankful. Let your whole life be one of gratitude and show it at every opportunity.

If you would like living in the House of Many Mansions, you have to make your reservations in advance.

TOFFEE GRAHAMS

24 graham crackers
2/3 c. melted butter
2/3 c. firmly packed brown sugar
1 c. pecans, chopped
1 pkg. semi-sweet chocolate chips (6 oz.)

Preheat oven to 350 degrees. Line jellyroll pan with graham crackers. Combine melted butter and sugar. Mix to blend. Spread over grahams. Sprinkle with nuts. Bake 10 to 12 minutes or until bubbly. Remove from oven, sprinkle evenly with chocolate chips. Cover pan with cookie sheet for 10 minutes to melt chocolate. Remove cookie sheet and spread chocolate evenly over crackers. Cool. Break apart into squares. Wrap and pack for lunch boxes.

These are good with the chocolate omitted. We serve them often at any party we may have. Everybody likes them.

CHRISTMAS BRUNCH JAM

3 c. fresh cranberries
1 (20 oz.) can crushed pineapple, undrained
1 c. peeled and diced cooking apple
3 c. sugar
1½ c. water
1 ¾ t. grated lemon peel
2 T. lemon juice

Combine all ingredients in a Dutch oven. Cook, uncovered, over medium-low heat, stirring frequently, until mixture registers 221 degrees on a candy thermometer (this will take about 1½ hours.)

Spoon hot cranberry mixture into hot sterilized jars, leaving ¼-inch headspace; cover at once with metal lids, and screw bands tight. Process in boiling-water bath 15 minutes. Yield: 5 pints.

OBSERVATIONS

Proverbs 12:25 "An anxious heart weighs a man down, but a kind word cheers him up."

All of the symptoms of cancer were there. The doctor was not very encouraging when he examined the patient. There was going to be a five day wait for all of the tests to get back from the pathologist.

What does a person do during this time and what does she think about? For one thing, she doesn't think very positively. With the way things were looking, there didn't seem to be much to think positively about.

I prayed more than usual. I got my priorities hurriedly straightened out.

At first there was a feeling of panic! Thoughts of family were uppermost in mind. These were selfish thoughts . . . like . . . wanting to see my grandchildren grow up. Then, as soon as these thoughts entered my mind, I had to tell myself that God had already granted my prayers of thirty years ago when our first son was born. At that time my constant prayer was to live to raise my own children . . . as I feel sure every mother prays.

Then there were thoughts of wanting to see our youngest son married and wondering who he would find as a suitable wife. And there were silly thoughts, like, would my husband bother to take his medication if I did not lay it out for him each morning. There were thoughts of friends. If death came, would anyone truly grieve or would the friends and acquaintances just think "that's too bad" and go on with their lives?

After the feeling of panic subsided somewhat, there was an attack of "poor me." There have been so many things happen during my lifetime that caused me to suffer, why couldn't I live to be 89, in reasonably good health, then die with a heart attack . . . during my sleep.

My husband was worried. He prayed with me and for me. Neither of us slept very well. The day was Saturday. A friend came by.

Maybe . . . before I go on . . . I should tell you my symptoms so that you can see I did have reason for much concern . . . and . . . perhaps some of you can gather encouragement from knowing about them. My doctor had found a mass in my left breast. He called it fibrocystic disease. He had me come to his office every 3 months for a pap smear of the clear fluid that drained from my breast. The tests had always come back negative. He told me that so long as the fluid was clear, there was usually no cause for alarm.

It had been about nine months since the mass was found and the drainage had started. On a Friday night, as I took off my bra, there were bloody stains inside the left cup. I put on my sleeping bra (which I began wearing when the trouble started) and went on to bed. The next morning there was evidence of the bloody drainage in my sleeping bra as well.

I called my doctor at home and asked him "what could cause the drainage from my left breast to become bloody other than turning cancerous? He said, "I take it this has happened to you?" I replied, weakly, "Yes." He said, "We can't do a thing until Monday. Come to the office Monday and we will take a smear. It will be Wednesday before we know for sure. But try not to worry."

Looming before my mind was, *5 DAYS, THEN I'LL KNOW.*

Now . . . back to the friend coming by. We had previously bought tickets to an Antique Show; she had come by for me. The only thing on my mind was, I didn't want to go. I wanted to stay at home. There was a feeling that every minute with my husband was very precious and that is where I wanted to be.

She blew the horn and I reluctantly went on out to get in the car and go with her. She was talking fast and furiously about a former male friend who had recently married (my friend is single). After we had gone about 2 miles, I interrupted her and said, "I may have cancer."

She said, "Really? Hmmmm." Then she went on with her conversation. I felt crushed.

I told three other close friends. Two of them reacted the way I thought they would . . . with real concern and love for a friend. They called each day to ask if by chance the report had come any sooner than expected. The other friend kept saying things like, "I feel sure it's nothing. You're just overly concerned. I'm sure it's nothing to worry about." As she would say this, I would think, "There is definitely something wrong; otherwise, I would never have gone in for tests."

I'm one of the fortunate ones. When the tests came back, there was no malignancy but a chronic infection that gave the same symptoms, and surgery was necessary to remove the infected mass.

As I thought back over those five days of waiting, not knowing whether or not I had cancer, I was able to observe the different reactions. Why do people react the way they do? Why do we? Why do I?

Few people know how to react to a difficult situation. It is my opinion that if one does not know how to react, the best thing to say is, "I'm so sorry, do you want to talk about it? Is there any way I can help you?" By saying something like this it will give the person an "in" if she wishes to talk about it.

I feel sure that most times when people act unconcerned, they really don't know how to react, so they don't say anything. This gives the impression that they are uncaring. End of observation. End of book.

SUNDAY DINNER

1 (7 oz.) box instant rice
1 can cream of mushroom soup
1 can cream of celery soup
1 fryer, cut up
1 envelope dried onion soup mix

Mix canned soups and pour over rice, spread in bottom of large casserole. Place pieces of chicken and sprinkle with onion soup. Cover and bake at 250-300 degrees for 2½ to 3 hours. Serves 8.

Serve this with baked fruit or fruit salad and a green vegetable. Delicious!

HAWAIIAN FUDGE

2½ c. sugar
1 small can crushed pineapple, drained
1 c. pecans
1 c. evaporated milk, undiluted
Few drops green food coloring

In large saucepan combine sugar, milk and pineapple. Bring to a boil over medium heat and cook until mixture reaches the soft ball stage. Remove from heat and add pecans and coloring. Let cool slightly; then beat until creamy. Pour into greased loaf pan, cool, and cut into squares. 18 squares.

STRAWBERRY BUTTER

1 (10 oz.) carton frozen strawberries, thawed
1 c. unsalted butter, softened
1/2 c. powdered sugar

Combine all ingredients in a mixing bowl; mix until blended and smooth. Store in refrigerator. Yield: 1 3/4 c.

Helps: Jelly in a squeeze bottle (like restaurants use for catsup or mustard) is easy for children to handle.

Use a colorful bed sheet as a washable picnic or party cloth.

A snap-style sweater clip can transform a napkin into a bib for our toddler when we visit restaurants or eat away from home.